Anne Stanesby is a solicitor. She has worked in private practice, in a Law Centre and for the organization Release. She is a member of the support group to the Citizens' Advice Bureau in Tooting Bec psychiatric hospital. She was on the collective which wrote *Trouble With The Law* (Pluto Press, 1978).

Anne Stanesby

Consumer Rights Handbook

Pluto Press

First published in 1986 by Pluto Press Limited,
The Works, 105a Torriano Avenue, London NW5 2RX
and Pluto Press Australia Limited, PO Box 199, Leichhardt,
New South Wales 2040, Australia. Also Pluto Press,
27 South Main Street, Wolfeboro, New Hampshire 03894-2069

7   6   5   4   3   2   1

90   89   88   87   86

Typeset by AKM Associates (UK) Limited,
Ajmal House, Hayes Road, Southall, London
Printed in Great Britain by Cox & Wyman Limited,
Reading, Berks.

British Library Cataloguing in Publication Data
Stanesby, Anne
   Consumer rights.——(Pluto Press workers' handbooks)
   1. Consumer protection——Law and
   legislation——Great Britain
   I. Title
   344.103'71   KD2204

ISBN 0 7453 0016   2

Contents

Note
This book is written for private consumers and not for people who are in business. Although some of the laws are the same, not all will be. If you want to know what your rights as a businessperson are you will have to look elsewhere. (See reading list on page 170).

1.

Introduction

The topic 'consumer rights' covers a wide area. Most people perform acts of consumption constantly throughout the day. We eat, travel, buy clothes, employ others to do things for us which we either cannot or have no time to do for ourselves, make telephone calls, visit the doctor and so on. The disasters that can result from an act of consumption are many and various, ranging in severity from personal injury to the loss of a few pounds. A consumer will certainly want to take action if the loss is serious but even in minor cases most people feel a sense of outrage coupled with a desire to do something about it.

Nowadays the consumer is in a strong position, whereas in the past purchasers were left largely to fend for themselves. In the last century the sale of adulterated products was rife and impecunious consumers were effectively powerless to protect themselves against exploitation. This century, however, a number of laws have been passed with the object of protecting the individual consumer. There are statutes regulating the sale of goods, services and credit, and traders now have extensive legal obligations imposed upon them. Evasion of those obligations by the use of small print or any other method is for the most part illegal, and businesspersons who do not fulfil their obligations to consumers can be sued in the civil courts or prosecuted by local authorities in the criminal courts. Traders have also been encouraged by the government to regulate themselves and to settle consumers' complaints on a voluntary basis.

However, laws are one thing and realities another. Consumers still get cheated, laws or no laws. Maybe this is because they do not realize what extensive legal rights they now have or because they are outmanoeuvred by wily tradespeople who know all the angles. In this book we set out both to inform consumers about their legal rights and to give practical advice about what to do if those rights are violated. It is a fact of life that most businesspersons do have more economic power than the average consumer but that does not mean that the consumer cannot win. The real life court cases quoted in the book demonstrate that.

It *is* possible to obtain redress if a trader cheats you and it need not cost you any or a lot of money to do so. As we shall show in this book, the law is there and consumers should take advantage of it.

About this book

For reasons of space we cannot cover every aspect of consumer rights but we have tried to deal with most of the problems the average consumer might come up against. We begin with some legal explanations which you are strongly advised to read and refer back to when necessary. They explain some general legal principles and legal terms which are vital to the understanding of what is said in the rest of the book.

The first three parts of the book set out what legal and other rights consumers have when buying goods, buying services and buying credit. The fourth part gives advice about what to do when these rights have been violated. We have tried to make the index as comprehensive as possible so if you have a problem about particular kinds of goods and services you should be able to tell by looking in the index whether they are separately covered. Even if not, the statement of general law given at the beginning of each of the three sections should give the reader enough ammunition to deal with the problem.

If the legal position is different from England and Wales in Scotland or Northern Ireland we shall state this either in the text or in a footnote.

Legal explanation

What is 'the law'?

The law is contained, most importantly, in legislation and secondly in decided court cases. If a unique problem occurs which is not covered by either then certain law textbooks, time-honoured customs and various other sources can be consulted.

Legislation

At various times throughout this book we shall be referring to Acts or statutes (both words mean the same thing). Acts of Parliament become law after they have been passed by both Houses of Parliament and have received the Royal Assent. An Act may come into force immediately or at a later date, or it may be introduced in stages. We will also be referring to Regulations or Orders. These are sometimes called 'delegated legislation' because when an Act has been passed by Parliament to deal with a particular situation, Parliament can at the same time and in the body of the Act, delegate to an official person the right to draw up Regulations to deal with details or future situation which it is not possible or appropriate to include in the main Act. When drafted, the Regulations are laid before Parliament and become law within a certain period of time, unless somebody objects. Regulations can only be drawn up when there is an Act of Parliament already in existence from which the right to make the particular Regulations derives.

An Act of Parliament may be passed as a result of an EEC Directive being adopted by the EEC Council of Ministers. The contents of such Directives must be introduced into the law of member states. It is left to the states concerned as to how they effect this but time limits are imposed.

In this book, so far as possible, when a legal right derives from an Act or Regulation we have given details of the legislation in question. We frequently give the section number and sometimes reproduce the actual wording, so aggrieved consumers can, when necessary, state the authority for the proposition they wish to put forward.

Decided court cases

Decisions made in court are an important source of law. Court decisions may be the only authority on a particular issue or they may be the authority that decides how a particular piece of legislation is to be interpreted, as it is not possible to legislate for every situation that might occur. Legislation can be passed to change the rule of law in a decided court case and to that extent court cases are subordinate to the rule of parliament. Courts must follow decisions made by courts superior in the hierarchy and they are also bound by decisions made by a court of the same level. To avoid a complete stalemate, however, the House of Lords, which is the highest court, can in certain circumstances decide not to follow a decision that it made previously.

As far as possible, when using an example to illustrate a point, we have tried to use a real life court case because these are a source of law in themselves. If there has not been a court case to illustrate the point in question then we have used fictional examples. If a real court case is used we have stated the name of the case, together with a date, various letters and a page number. The latter denote where the case can be found in official law report books.

Crimes and civil wrongs

There are two sorts of court system: the civil and the criminal. The criminal court system deals with behaviour considered so heinous that the state should intervene, and, if found guilty, punish the offender. In criminal cases, therefore, the state usually prosecutes the matter. (In theory private persons can prosecute but this is not easy and is very rare.) There are various sorts of bad behaviour in the field of consumer affairs that are crimes and we shall be detailing these. If a criminal prosecution takes place it is possible that as part of the punishment the offending trader will be ordered to pay compensation to the aggrieved consumer.

The civil court system deals with disputes which citizens have with each other. If the wrong which a consumer has suffered does not amount to a crime and if redress through the courts is required, the consumer will have to take the initiative and start off the case. Civil wrongs in this area will be either breaches of contract or torts (delicts in Scotland). We shall explain below what a contract consists of; a person cannot sue another for breach of contract unless she was a party to the contract in question. This rule can adversely affect those who received the goods in question as a gift because they did not 'contract' with the trader. A tort or delict consists of a breach of duty imposed by the law, which is owed to persons generally whether or not they made a contract with the trader.

Of course wrongs do not have to be resolved by court proceedings and in Part IV we shall set out various alternative ways in which the matter might be settled. Also, one result of the pressure put on businesses to regulate their own affairs is that sometimes a consumer can obtain redress even though the conduct complained of is not actually against the law.

Contracts

When a consumer buys goods in a shop or pays for a service a contract has been made. A contract is in effect a bargain that is legally enforceable through the courts, but it must contain certain elements in order to have legal effect. These are briefly as follows:

- One side has to make a serious offer to the other, i.e. it must be obvious that the person making the offer is prepared to be legally obligated if the other person agrees to what is proposed. (The courts have decided that displays of goods in shop windows and advertisements are not usually offers in the legal sense. They are instead what are called 'invitations to treat' (see p. 39). The person making the offer can withdraw it at any time before the other person intimates that they want to accept. If the offer is withdrawn in time the person making it cannot be held to it.
- The other person must accept the offer unconditionally. If s/he makes new conditions s/he has not accepted the offer but has made a counter offer which must in turn be accepted by the other side before the bargain can be finalized. The acceptance must usually be communicated to the other side by words or conduct. If the acceptance is by post it takes effect from the time of posting.

- Except in Scotland the offer and acceptance must be accompanied by what is called 'consideration'. This is a benefit conferred or a detriment suffered by one or other of the parties to the contract and so is wider than just pure cash. If the whole thing is just a matter of charity the courts will not intervene. In Scotland a charitable contract can be enforced but only if its existence can be proved in writing.
- Contracts for the purchase of goods or services for cash do not have to be in writing to be enforceable. They can be verbal or, if in writing, do not have to be in any particular form. Credit contracts, however, usually do have to be in writing and must comply with strict formalities.

Unenforceable contracts

A consumer can only enforce a contract if s/he was the person who entered into it. Sometimes though the contract cannot be enforced by the trader against the consumer. This could occur if the consumer did not have the legal 'capacity' to make the contract. Three categories of persons might not have the necessary capacity: minors (and pupils in Scotland), the mentally ill and drunkards.

Minors

A minor is anyone aged under 18 but in Scotland there is the additional juvenile category of pupil. Pupils are girls aged under 12 and boys under 14, and they cannot enter into valid contracts. Except in Scotland, minors cannot do so either. In Scotland minors may enter into contracts, but if they have a 'curator' who did not consent the contract may not be enforceable against them. There are some exceptions to the general position.

If minors or pupils buy goods which are 'necessaries' they must pay a reasonable price for them. This is stated in Section 3 of the Sale of Goods Act 1979. The statute states that necessaries are 'goods suitable to the condition in life of the minor . . . and to his actual requirements at the time of sale and delivery'.

■ An undergraduate went up to study at Trinity College, Cambridge. The student's father was an architect of good position who equipped his son with proper clothes in which to go to university. Once there the son was supplied with various articles of clothing which included 11 fancy waistcoats, 'clothing of an extravagant and ridiculous style having regard to the position of the boy', according to one judge. The 'boy' failed to pay the bill and the court held that he did not have to. The fancy waistcoats were not 'necessaries'; he had enough clothes as it was. (Nash v Inman 1908 2 KB (CA) 1)

Also, except in Scotland a minor buying services can be forced to pay if the service is 'necessary', similar criteria being applied. Medical treatment and legal advice, for example, would usually be considered 'necessary'.

If money is lent to a minor the minor cannot be forced to pay it back unless the money was lent to buy necessaries for which, once again, a 'reasonable' price must be paid. (In Scotland, money lent to pupils and minors and spent for their benefit has to be paid back to the extent of the value of the benefit received.) As will be seen later, the Consumer Credit Act provides that it is a criminal offence to send credit circulars to minors and to take a pawn ticket from one.

Mentally ill persons

Consumers who are so mentally ill when entering into a contract that they cannot understand the nature of what they are undertaking can try to get out of it later, but they will have to prove that the other person knew of their confused state of mind. When it comes to necessary goods, they are in the same position as minors under Section 3 of the Sale of Goods Act. (In Scotland contracts with insane persons are of no effect except when buying necessary goods.)

Drunkards

If consumers are so drunk when making a contract that they don't know what they are doing, and if they can prove the other person was aware of their state, they can try to set the contract aside. Again, if what they bought were necessary goods, Section 3 applies. (In Scotland drunk persons must additionally repudiate the contract as soon as they recover their senses and realize what they've done.)

What are the terms of a contract?

The terms of a contract, i.e. the bases on which the deal was made, may be set out in a written document, agreed verbally between the consumer and the trader, or may be obvious from the surrounding circumstances. Additionally, an Act of Parliament may provide that a term be compulsorily included in the contract regardless of the wishes of the trader. The Sale of Goods Act, for instance, stipulates that there is to be an implied term in most contracts for the sale of goods that the goods sold be of 'merchantable quality'.

If a term of the contract is not adhered to then a breach of contract is said to have occurred. The consumer's remedies for the breach of contract depend partly on the status of the term which has been breached.

Conditions and warranties

Conditions and warranties are legal expressions to describe the terms of the contract (except in Scotland). A condition is an important term and a warranty is a minor term. If a condition has been broken, the consumer can 'rescind' the contract, i.e. get out of it altogether and/or claim damages. If a warranty has been broken only damages can be claimed. A term is a condition either because the contract says it is or because it has been put into the contract by an Act of Parliament which says that it is or because it is obviously an important element in the deal.

In Scotland terms are not described in this way. If a term is 'material' and is breached then the consumer can rescind the contract and/or claim damages. If the term is not material then only damages can be claimed.

Damages

If a breach of contract has taken place damages can be awarded with the object of putting the wronged person into the same position as if the contract had been carried out as it should have been. Damages can be claimed for obvious losses arising from the breach and for those losses which 'may reasonably be supposed to have been in the contemplation of both parties, at the time they made the contract as to the probable result of the breach of it'. (This was stated in the case of Hadley v Baxendale 1854 9 Ex 341.) A consumer can therefore claim damages both for losses that arise naturally from the breach of contract and for those the parties should obviously have anticipated. A consumer must 'mitigate' their loss, i.e. make the best of a bad situation, and, if there is any dispute about value, the market price as at the time of the breach of contract will be taken as a yardstick.

If a tort or delict has occurred then damages can be awarded with the object of putting the aggrieved person in the same position as if they had not suffered the wrong in question. Obviously this is a somewhat academic exercise if personal injury has occurred. You cannot give someone a leg back; all you can try to do is to work out what is fair compensation for such a terrible occurrence. Calculating damages for personal injury is a highly technical affair and advice should always be taken. Damages can also be awarded not just for the loss but also for the pain and suffering, loss of earnings and possible future loss. Additionally, if the injury gives more trouble in the future than had been originally contemplated the injured person can go back to the court and claim more money.

Part I

Buying Goods

Buying consumer goods is normally a pleasurable experience but sometimes things do go wrong. The goods bought may not live up to the consumer's expectations or there may be other problems, such as late delivery. In this section we set out what legal and other rights of redress a consumer has when purchasing goods. The consumer may, for instance, have a right to sue the seller in the civil court, the seller may be liable to prosecution in the criminal courts or the consumer may be able to complain to various authorities about the seller's activities.

If you have not read *Legal explanation* yet, then you may well need to do so in order to understand everything in this section. For example, many consumer rights are based on the law of contract and if you do not understand the basic principles some of what follows may be confusing. You should also refer back to *Legal explanation* for the meaning of 'damages' and 'condition' and 'warranty'.

Practically all the legal rights of redress described are available only to the person who actually bought the goods. If the goods were given to you then you have very few legal rights at all. Where someone other than the purchaser can take legal action it will be specifically stated. Most of the legal rights of redress described are only enforceable against the actual seller of the goods and not the manufacturer. Where the manufacturer can also be sued this will be specifically stated. Both these situations arise because of the principles of the law of contract.

The legal rights of redress described are the maximum available to the buyer. Of course you do not have to insist on enforcing your rights to the full if you do not want to. For example, if it's stated that 'the purchaser is entitled to a full refund', there is nothing to stop you accepting a replacement item instead if you would rather do so. But you cannot be forced to accept anything less than your maximum legal entitlement unless *you* want to. For example, if goods purchased are not up to the legal standard required, as described in the 'shoddy goods' section then you cannot be forced to accept a credit note to buy something else at the shop in question if you would rather have your money returned to you.

In addition to any legal rights of redress available, an aggrieved consumer may wish to report a trader to a trading association where possible (details later). Note that a consumer can also consider reporting *any* errant trader to the local authority's Trading Standards Department (See p. 175).

Consumers' rights when purchasing goods and services together are dealt with in Part II, and Part III deals with consumers' rights when purchasing goods on hire purchase or by other forms of credit.

1.

Buying goods in trade premises

Sales talk

Here we deal with the effect of any words spoken during the course of a consumer purchase. Often, of course, goods are purchased without a word being said. The customer selects the item, goes straight to the till, pays for it and leaves. Sometimes, however, purchasers may want some information about the product before deciding whether or not to buy it. They may want to know what qualities it has, for example whether it is waterproof or simply what it is made of or what size it is. What is said could later turn out to be untrue or incorrect. Sometimes the customer does not intend to ask the seller any questions or even to buy anything but is approached by a salesperson who persuades them to make a purchase which they later regret.

The buyer who falls victim to sales talk would have a legal remedy in certain circumstances but not in others. The law in this area is not easy to understand but, as a general rule, if something of importance was said about the product before the purchase took place and this statement later turns out to be untrue or incorrect there is usually something a purchaser can do. Below we set out the possible legal remedies a buyer might have when misled by sales talk.

Misrepresentation

Buyers have some legal rights when lured into making purchases because of incorrect statements (called 'misrepresentations' by lawyers). It may be possible to sue for breach of contract if it can be established that the words spoken were meant to be taken seriously and to form a term of the contract. Do not waste too much energy trying to work out if what has happened is a breach of contract or not because there is a separate legal right to sue for the wrong of misrepresentation.

Not all misrepresentations are 'actionable', i.e. giving rise to a right to sue in the civil court. Anything said after the item has been bought is irrelevant: the misrepresentation must have taken place *before* the item was purchased. Also, the customer must have been influenced to some extent by the statement. If what was said made no difference to the decision to purchase then there would be no right to sue for misrepresentation. The statement must also be one that an average person would take seriously, so sales 'puffs', e.g. 'whiter than white', are not covered.

If a breach of contract has taken place the consumer's remedies depend on whether the words amounted to a condition or a warranty or were material (see *Legal explanation*). If a 'mere' misrepresentation occurred then the consumer who does not hesitate too long and can return the goods unchanged, may 'rescind the contract' (i.e. set it aside) and get all his/her money back. If the misrepresentation was made dishonestly ('fraudulent misrepresentation') or carelessly ('negligent misrepresentation'), the consumer can also claim damages. (The right to damages for negligent misrepresentation is based on the Misrepresentation Act 1967 in England, Wales and Northern Ireland.)

■ A man bought a secondhand car. The dealer had said to him *before* he purchased it: 'It's a good little bus. I would stake my life on it. You will have no trouble with it.' Precisely one week later the purchaser was injured when the car came into collision with a lorry. It transpired that the collision was caused by the failure of the drag link joint of the car's steering, which was in a dangerous condition, and the purchaser sued for damages. The dealer's lawyer tried to argue, amongst other things, that the words said were not meant to be taken seriously and were just sales talk, mere puffing. The court disagreed and decided that what was said amounted to a term in the contract to the effect that the car was in good condition and reasonably safe and fit to use on the highway. The purchaser won the case. (Andrews v Hopkinson (1957) 1 QB 229)

Misdescription

The Sale of Goods Act 1979 protects a buyer who has purchased something which the seller has inaccurately described. Section 13(1) of the Act states: 'Where there is a contract for the sale of goods by description there is an implied condition that the goods will correspond with the description.' This means that when a consumer buys goods on trade premises the Act inserts into the contract between buyer and seller a condition to the effect that the goods must comply with any description the trader has applied to them. The seller cannot evade this obligation by any method. The misdescription must have occurred *before* the purchase took place. If the seller tries to argue that shop purchases are not 'sales by description' then you can state with confidence that they are as this is clearly set out in the Act (Section 13(3)).

If a breach of Section 13 has taken place then the buyer will usually have the right to a complete refund but this right can be lost by delay (see p. 33 for more details). The customer can also claim damages in addition to or instead of a refund in those situations where the right to a refund has been lost.

■ A woman goes into a shop and looks at a shirt. The label does not say what the shirt is made of so she makes enquiries from the salesperson who says, 'Oh, that's made of pure cotton, very good value.' If this statement later turns out to be inaccurate then the shop has breached Section 13 of the Sale of Goods Act. The buyer could probably also sue for misrepresentation.

Criminal prosecution

Apart from any rights to sue in the civil court for misrepresentation or breach of Section 13 of the Sale of Goods Act, it might also be possible that the seller who has made an inaccurate or untrue statement has committed a criminal offence and could be prosecuted by the local authority. A consumer might benefit if the prosecution were to be successful because of the criminal courts' power to award compensation (see p. 199).

Section 1(1) of the Trade Description Act 1968 states that a criminal offence has been committed if anyone 'in the course of a trade or business, (a) applies a false trade description to any goods, or (b) supplies or offers to supply any goods to which a false trade description is applied'. The word 'applies' covers a wide range of activities and includes oral statements.

Section 2 sets out a list of things which it is criminal to describe falsely.
(a) quantity, size or gauge;
(b) method of manufacture, production, processing or reconditioning;
(c) composition;

(d) fitness for purpose, strength, performance, behaviour or accuracy;
(e) any other physical characteristics;
(f) testing by any person and results thereof;
(g) approval by any person or conformity with a type approved by any person;
(h) place or date of manufacture, production, processing or reconditioning;
(i) person by whom manufactured, produced, processed or reconditioned;
(j) other history including previous ownership or use.

Under Section 12 it is also an offence falsely to represent that goods were supplied to or approved by the Royal Family!

There are various defences available to traders. They may be cleared if they can prove:

(a) that the commission of the offence was due to a mistake or to reliance on information supplied to him or to the act or default of another person. An accident or some other cause beyond his control; and

(b) that he took all reasonable precautions and exercised all due diligence to avoid the commission of such an offence by himself or any person under his control. (Section 24(1))

Such defences would not be available in a civil court case.

■ A woman goes into a shop looking for a coat: she sees one she likes. While she is wondering whether to buy it the salesperson deliberately lies to her and says: 'It's a lovely coat, isn't it? They supply just this brand of coat to the Royal Family, you know.'

This statement does not influence the woman at all although she momentarily considers not buying the coat on principle. The salesperson could be prosecuted under the Trade Descriptions Act for telling lies about the coat's royal connections. However, were the consumer to purchase the coat she could not later sue for misrepresentation because the false statement did not influence her in any way.

Also note that it is a criminal offence to sell to a purchaser's prejudice any food which is not of the nature, substance or quality demanded by the purchaser. This offence is covered by the Food Act 1984 (England and Wales), the Food and Drugs (Scotland) Act 1956 and Food and Drugs Act (Northern Ireland) 1958. Under the Weights and Measures Acts it is a criminal offence to make an oral or written misrepresentation about the quantity of goods sold.

Sales pressure

Provided nothing that is actually untrue or inaccurate has been said about the product, consumers who have simple been talked into buying something they didn't really want have no legal remedy on that basis alone. However, a buyer who was under 18, mentally ill or drunk at the time of purchase might have some limited right of redress if the product was not a necessary one for him/her to have. (See *Legal explanation*, p. 6.)

If the salesperson's behaviour has been particularly bad and a complaint direct to the shop does not resolve the matter, it is worth complaining further to the relevant trading association if the shop is a member of one and/or to the local authority or Office of Fair Trading (see p. 175).

Sales print

Even if nothing is actually said when a customer purchases an item there may be something in writing. Purchasers could have read something in a newspaper or in a shop window and been induced or encouraged by what the advertisement states to buy the product later. They may subsequently discover that the item does not have all the attributes the advertisement claimed. Possibly, too, the label or packaging on the product may bear no resemblance to what is inside or the seller may have omitted to give the purchasers all the information they are entitled by law to receive. Below we set out what rights consumers have in these situations.

The seller may also have given the purchaser a standard form contract or a manufacturer's guarantee. Of what use are such documents to the purchaser if the product goes wrong? And what is the position of a customer who returns to a shop to complain about a faulty product only to be told that the trader cannot be held responsible because, for example, there is a notice to that effect behind the door which the customer did not even notice?

Advertisements

If an advertisement contains a statement about a product which turns out to be untrue or inaccurate then there are a number of possible courses of action an aggrieved purchaser could take.

If the advertisement was displayed by the person who sold you the goods then the following options are available:

Sue the seller for misrepresentation. The rules are the same as for the spoken word (see p. 15) but the purchaser will have the added advantage that when something is in writing its existence is easier to prove. Don't forget that sales 'puffs' are *not* actionable misrepresentations.

Sue the seller for breach of Section 13 of the Sale of Goods Act if the advertisement misdescribes the product (see p. 16). The rules are the same as for the spoken word.

■ A secondhand Rolls Royce was advertised as having 'the full history available'. The would-be purchaser checked and found there was indeed a service record in the car. After he had bought the car the buyer discovered the service record related to a completely different vehicle. The court decided the seller had breached the provisions of Section 13 of the Sale of Goods Act as the car had been misdescribed in the advertisement. The purchaser won the case. Alton House Garages (Bromley) Ltd v Monk QBD 31 July 1981, not reported but referred to in *Consumer Law Encyclopedia* (Sweet & Maxwell) 3-E 255

Ask the local authority to prosecute the seller for an offence under the Trade Description Act. The rules are the same as for the spoken word, so see p. 17.

■ A secondhand car dealer put into a paper an advertisement which included the words: 'Showroom condition throughout is the only way to describe this 1968 Austin 1100 Estate.' A consumer saw the advertisement and later bought the car. Three weeks later the purchaser took the car to another garage for a check-up. They discovered various defects and advised her to contact her local authority's Consumer Protection Department. She did so and the local authority arranged for a consulting engineer to examine the vehicle. The engineer's report listed many defects and the dealer was prosecuted for falsely describing the car in the advertisement. He tried to escape by arguing that the advertisement could not amount to a false trade description as it was just a trade puff, being indiscriminate praise and not an assertion of verifiable fact. He was found guilty. (Hawkins v Smith (1978) CLR P 578)

If the advertisement was not displayed by the person who sold you the goods but by somebody else, e.g. the manufacturer, then the legal position is more complicated and there is not room to go into it fully here. Because the purchaser has usually made a contract only with the seller, buyers' rights to sue the manufacturer for misleading them with an advertisement are curtailed. However, it might be possible to sue the manufacturer for breach of what is known as a 'collateral contract'. Depending on how the advertisement is worded it might be possible to argue that there is a contract between a manufacturer advertiser and the consumer who bought the product from a retailer. This is a tricky area of law and no one should start a legal action on this basis without getting advice first.

■ The manufacturers of a medical product called the carbolic smokeball put an advertisement into the newspaper which said amongst other things: '£100 reward will be paid by the Carbolic Smokeball Company to any person who contracts the increasing epidemic influenza, colds or any disease caused by taking cold after having used the vall three times daily for two weeks according to the printed directions supplied with each ball. £1,000 is deposited with the Alliance Bank, Regent Street showing our sincerity in the matter.' A consumer bought a carbolic smokeball at a chemist's, used it as directed and got flu anyway. The manufacturers refused to pay her the promised £100 and so she sued them for it. The court held the company must keep their promise. The advertisement was phrased in such a way that the public would expect them to do so. There was a collateral contract between the manufacturer advertiser and the consumer. Suggestions that there could be no contract because the consumer had not provided 'consideration' were rejected as the inconvenience of sniffing the carbolic smokeball three times a day was consideration enough. The consumer won the case. (Carllil v Carbolic Smoke Ball Co. (1893) 1 QB 256)

Alternatively, the purchaser could ask the local authority to prosecute the manufacterer for an offence under the Trade Descriptions Act. Undoubtedly this is the better option. The manufacturer is liable to prosecution in the same way as retailers are (see p. 17). In addition, anyone who puts out an advertisement which falsely describes food or is calculated to mislead as to the nature or substance or quality of the food can be prosecuted.

Purchasers who have no legal remedy but still feel that an advertiser of goods has behaved improperly can complain about it. Unless the advertisement was on the television or radio (see below) the body to complain to is the Advertising Standards Authority (ASA), Brook House, 2–16 Torrington Place, London WC1E 7H. Tel: 01–580 5555. The ASA publishes the British Code of Advertising Practice, a set of rules to which advertisers should adhere. The code states as a general principle that all advertisements must be legal, decent, honest and truthful and prepared with a sense of responsibility to the consumer and to society. Advertisements should not exploit a consumer's lack of experience or knowledge; factual claims about a product must be capable of substantiation; testimonials must be genuine and the advertisement should not contain anything that is likely to mislead the consumer about the product advertised. There are special rules about particular types of advertisements, such as those aimed at children and those dealing with health claims, cigarettes and alcohol. The ASA state that if they consider that a complaint is well founded they will ensure that the advertisement is amended or withdrawn completely. They claim that if the advertiser will not co-coperate the ASA can resort to adverse publicity or deprivation of advertising space. The ASA's code does not have the force of law and is an example of an industry allegedly controlling itself.

If misled or offended by an advertisement on television or radio the person to write to is the Deputy Controller of Advertising, Independent Broadcasting Authority (IBA), 70 Brompton Road, London SW3 1EY. Tel: 01–584 7011. The IBA was set up by the Broadcasting Act of 1981 and has a statutory duty to draw up a code of practice for television and radio advertisements and to make sure this code is adhered to. The code is similar in content to the one published by the ASA but in addition the use of technical devices which might influence audiences without their realizing it is banned and special techniques or substitute materials must not be used 'unless the resultant picture presents a fair and reasonable impression of the product or its effects and is not such as to mislead'. The IBA is supposed to monitor advertisement *before* they are broadcast to make sure they are not in breach of the code. However, in what they might well regard as the unlikely event of an individual demonstrating that an offensive or misleading advertisement had slipped through the net, they say it would be removed or amended.

Packaging, labels, price marking and other descriptions

If packaging, labels or notices describing goods contain information which is untrue or incorrect then there are a number of possible courses of action an aggrieved purchaser could take:

● Sue the seller for misrepresentation.
● Sue the seller for breach of Section 13 of the Sale of Goods Act if the product has been misdescribed.
● Ask the local authority to prosecute the seller for an offence under the Trade Descriptions Act.

The rules are the same as set out on pp. 15–18.

■ An egg producer who had been selling eggs described as 'free range' was successfully prosecuted under the Trade Descriptions Act. The court stated that for the description 'free range eggs' to be accurate, the hens needed not only regular daytime access to land but that this access should be at a density of about 150 birds per acre with freedom to roam widely over it. The hens must derive a significant part of their food from nature permanently and not from time to time. This part of their diet had to be an integral part of their routine. (Reported in *Consumer Law Encyclopedia* (Sweet & Maxwell) at p. 118 l. 450)

It is also against the law to make misleading statements about prices. Section 11 of the Trade Descriptions Act states that it is a criminal offence for a trader to make 'false indications' about the price of goods offered for sale. For instance, it is an offence for a trader falsely to state that goods are being sold at a price which is less than that recommended by the manufacturer or to make any false suggestions to the effect that the goods will be sold for less than the actual price that will in fact be charged. In addition, the Price Marking (Bargain Offers) Order 1979 forbids most sorts of 'double pricing', i.e. comparing a price offered by a trader with some other price with the object of putting the former in a favourable light. The following types of comparison, for example, are not allowed:

● Worth or value claims, e.g. worth £10 – our price £8. In one court case the price of jewellery was compared with 'insurance value' and the shop was found guilty. (Reported in Sweet and Maxwell, *Consumer Law Encyclopedia* at 2:493.)

● Comparisons with a previous price offered by the trader are not allowed unless the goods in question have been on display at the previous higher price for at least 28 consecutive days in the last 6 months at that shop or another branch and at least one sale has taken place at either location at the previous higher price. In one court case there was a so-called 'half price' sale and a comparison made with so-called 'normal prices' but in fact the two were the same. The shop was found guilty. (Reported as above in *Consumer Law Encyclopedia.*)

● Where certain types of goods are being sold no comparison at all may be made between the trader's offered price and the recommended or manufacturer's retail price. The goods covered are listed in the Order. The list is long and includes beds, electric domestic appliances such as refrigerators and kettles, consumer electronic goods, carpets, furniture and various other items.

Traders are allowed to make the following types of price comparison:

● Introductory offers are allowed but only if the time for which they will last is specified clearly.
● Traders can compare their prices with that of a competitor but *only* if they name the competitor in question.
● Traders can compare prices if trading terms are different, e.g. if a lower price is offered to cash customers.
● Traders can compare prices if the goods are now in a different condition, e.g. shop-soiled, or if a different quantity is now being offered.
● Traders can have a different price for certain categories of people, e.g. concessionary prices can be offered to old age pensioners.
● Traders can compare prices if other goods or services are now being offered with the main item being sold.

Any other sorts of 'double pricing' are not permitted.

The Prices Act 1974 states that when certain types of goods are sold the price *must* be marked or displayed. Covered by this provision are, for instance, meat and fish, fruit and vegetables, prepacked milk being sold in vending machines, cheese, food and drink being sold on the premises and petrol. We haven't room to list everything, so ask your local authority if you want more details (see p. 166).

In addition, since January 1982 certain types of goods have had to have marked on them their country of origin. This might interest those who wish to boycott the products of certain regimes. Products covered include most textiles, clothing, footwear, cutlery and domestic electrical appliances. Once again, ask your local authority for comprehensive details. The relevant legislation is the Trade Descriptions (Origin Marking) (Miscellaneous Goods) Order 1981.

Finally, anyone who gives, displays or attaches to food sold by them a label which falsely describes the food or is calculated to mislead as to the nature, substance or quality of the food can be prosecuted (see p. 18 for the relevant Acts). Under the Weights and Measures Acts anyone who sells short weight can be prosecuted as can those who sell goods with false statements attached to them.

Standard form contracts and guarantees

Each time a consumer purchases something s/he makes a contract with the seller. The contract does not have to be in writing and usually isn't when things are bought in shops. However, it is worth knowing where you stand if it is. A written contract does not have to be in any particular form. It may look like a contract or it may be contained in a receipt or invoice. Something in writing will nearly always take precedence over the spoken word. Therefore if the seller tells you one thing about a product but there is something in writing, say a receipt, which says different, the court would take more notice of the receipt than what you say the seller said to you. Purchasers should therefore read anything given to them in writing *very* carefully and should not hesitate to delete things they do not want to agree to or add what they want included. If there is a term in the contract to the purchaser's advantage which the seller does not adhere to, the purchaser should be able to sue for breach of contract. Obviously, having written evidence of what was agreed puts the buyer in a stronger position. A seller who has breached a contract term would have to give the buyer a refund plus damages or just damages depending on whether the term was a condition or a warranty (or of material importance in Scotland).

If there is a term to the seller's advantage in the contract which is particularly unfair, the law may operate to exclude it (see *Fine print*, below) but this does not mean that you should not read the piece of writing very carefully.

If the agreement between you and the seller is described as a 'guarantee' it is still legally a contract and the same rules apply. If you are given a manufacturer's guarantee then legally the position might be different. Whether the promises contained in the guarantee could be enforced through the courts would depend on all the circumstances and the terms of the guarantee itself. No one should start a court case off on the basis of a manufacturer's guarantee without getting advice first. In practice you can hope that the manufacturer will honour the guarantee voluntarily and if they do so the consumer may end up with a better deal than that given by the strict letter of the law. This is because manufacturers are sometimes prepared to guarantee products for some years and, as will be seen under *Shoddy goods*, it is doubtful if the she/he could be held legally responsible for something that breaks down some years after purchase. Also, those who are given an item as a present might be able to take advantage of a guarantee whereas they have very few legal rights in relation to bad quality goods. If a manufacturer refuses to honour the terms of a guarantee and you discover they belong to a trading association, it is well worth complaining to that trading association about what has occurred. Particularly unfair terms in guarantee will be struck out by the law but still the document should be read carefully.

Fine print

At one time exclusion or exemption clauses were widely used by traders as a method of evading their responsibilities to consumers. Traders would put up a notice in their shop or slip a clause into a contract or guarantee disclaiming all responsibility for shoddy or dangerous goods. Now legislation provides that most of these clauses are to have no or a restricted effect when consumer transactions take place and if traders put up notices suggesting that they *do* have the right to evade their responsibilities then *they* can be prosecuted in the criminal courts. Note that if consumers purchase goods which are normally sold to business customers only, e.g. building materials, they might be treated in law as if they actually were trade customers in which case the position is different. If a trader tries this, take advice (see pp. 165–71).

The Unfair Contract Terms Act 1977 states that some exclusion clauses are not to have any effect at all and others have effect only if they are considered to be 'reasonable'. The following types of exclusion clause have no effect at all:*

- Provisions contained in manufacturers' guarantees which state that the makers cannot be held responsible for loss or damage which has resulted from a consumer using goods which are defective because of the manufacturer's negligence.
- Exclusion clauses by which traders seek to evade certain provisions of the Sale of Goods Act are invalid if the customer is a consumer. The provisions in question are Section 12 (see p. 59) whereby the seller is assumed to have the right to sell the goods, Section 13 (see p. 16) whereby goods must not be misdescribed and Section 14 (see pp. 29–33) which deals with quality standards. Any attempt by a trader to evade the provisions of these sections will be of no effect where a consumer sale is involved.
- Exclusion clauses by which traders seek to avoid responsibility for death or injury caused by their negligence are of no effect. Death or injury could result from the use of dangerous goods (see pp. 34–9) or could occur if a customer had an accident whilst on the trader's premises (see p. 41)

The following types of exclusion clause are effective only if a court would consider them to be 'reasonable':

- Any clause in a contract with a consumer in which the trader tries to evade responsibility for (a) not sticking to the agreed terms of the contract; (b) performing the contract in a substantially different way; and (c) not performing his/her side of the contract at all.
- Any provision by which a trader tries to evade responsibility for misrepresentation is of no effect unless reasonable. This is actually stated in the Misrepresentation Acts (which do not apply in Scotland) but the Acts also state that the test of what is reasonable is the same as the one set out below.

---

* In Scotland the Act only applies to exclusion clauses contained in a contract. In England, Wales and Northern Ireland exclusion clauses contained in notices which are not part of the actual contract can also be rendered non-effective by these provisions.

- Exclusion clauses by which traders seek to avoid responsibility for economic loss or damage caused by their negligence.

The Unfair Contract Terms Act sets out a number of criteria which are to be considered when deciding if a contract term is reasonable. The most relevant are the following:

- The relative strength of the trader's and consumer's bargaining positions.
- Any inducement offered to the consumer to agree to the exclusion clause.
- Whether the consumer knew or should have known about the existence of the clause. This would be particularly relevant if the clause was contained in extremely small print or, for example, in an obscure little notice at the back of a dimly lit shop. (See case on p. 70 which relates to a British Rail exclusion clause which the court decided was not reasonable.)

Outlawing the use of exclusion clauses would be of little practical effect if traders were permitted to mislead consumers into believing that such clauses *could* still be used effectively. The Consumer Transactions (Restrictions on Statements) Order 1976 provides that traders who do attempt to mislead consumers by such methods can be prosecuted in the criminal courts.

Article 3 of this Order states that traders must not state or suggest that they are entitled to sell goods which contravene Section 13 and 14 of the Sale of Goods Act (which deal with misdescription and quality, see pp. 16 and 29–33). Traders are guilty if the offending statement is displayed in trade premises, published in an advertisement, placed on the goods themselves, or on their container or contained in a document given to the consumer when they buy the item.

Article 4 of this Order states that traders must make it clear to consumers that whatever compensation the trader is voluntarily prepared to offer if goods bought turn out to be unsatisfactory, customers may still insist on their full legal rights if they so wish. Traders who offer alternative deals by means of a statement on the goods themselves or their container, or one contained in a document given to the consumer at the time of purchase, are guilty *unless* there is a conspicuous notice nearby to say that the consumer's statutory rights are not affected. You have probably seen many such notices in well-known chain stores.

Article 5 of the Order imposes similar restrictions on manufacturers. If they put a statement on goods or on containers offering some sort of compensation if things go wrong when they too are guilty of an offence if they do not at the same time make it clear that the purchaser's statutory rights are not affected.

Traders have been found guilty for displaying notices saying: 'No cash refunds', 'All sale goods bought as seen. No refunds or exchanges can be made', 'We willingly exchange goods but regret no money can be refunded.' A car dealer was also successfully prosecuted for using a rubber stamp on a used car sales invoice which stated, 'This vehicle is sold without warranty.' A store committed an offence by giving a consumer a document which stated, 'Purchased as seen.' (All reported in Sweet and Maxwell, *Consumer Law Encyclopedia* at p. 2–305/1.)

Shoddy goods

Regardless of what may or may not have been said or written before a purchase takes place, consumers may well be dissatisfied with a product they have purchased because that product has not lived up to the expectations they personally had of it. The article might never work at all or it may not perform as well as the purchaser thinks it should. The product may have been bought with a specific purpose in mind and may not prove to be up to what is required. The defect in it may be obvious the day after purchase or may not be discovered till some months afterwards.

In the absence of any verbal or written agreement the old idea of *caveat emptor* ('buyer beware') still applies. However, the Sale of Goods Act 1979 sets out certain minimum standards of quality to which sellers must adhere. These are set out in Section 14 of the Act and, as already explained under *Fine print* on p. 26, any attempt by a trader to evade these obligations by the use of an exclusion clause is of no effect against a consumer and might leave the trader liable to a criminal prosecution.

Merchantable quality

Section 14(2) of the Sale of Goods Act states that where a trader sells goods '. . . there is an implied condition that the goods supplied under the contract are of *merchantable quality*'. The expression 'merchantable quality' has had a long history in the law courts and is far more relevant to commercial transactions than it is to consumer purchases. Section 14(6) attempts to explain what 'merchantable quality' means: 'Goods of any kind are of merchantable quality if they are as fit for the purpose/s for which goods of that kind are commonly bought as it is reasonable to expect having regard to any description applied to them, the price (if relevant) and all other relevant circumstances.'

The Act also states that there are two situations where the buyer is *not* protected by this condition. Section 14(2) says the buyer is not protected: '(a) as regards defects specifically drawn to the buyer's attention before the contract is made or (b) if the buyer examines the goods before the contract is made as regards defects which that examination ought to reveal.' This means that if purchasers are told about a defect before they buy something they cannot later claim compensation in respect of *that* defect. Also, if purchasers inspect a product before they buy it they cannot later claim compensation for any defect they ought to have noticed whilst making their inspection.

With those two exceptions the buyer does have some rights of redress if the goods purchased are not of merchantable quality, i.e. not up to the standard which could reasonably be expected taking all relevant circumstances into account. Very minor defects are not covered under this section and unfortunately the point at which a defect becomes sufficiently major to render a product 'unmerchantable' is incapable of precise definition. In one court case it was suggested that the test should be whether a buyer fully acquainted with all the facts (i.e. a buyer who knew about hidden defects as well as obvious ones) would have agreed to buy the goods in that condition without asking for a price reduction or other special term. (Lord Dixon in Australian Knitting Mills v Grant (1933) CLR 387, 418)

■ A brand new power boat sank within 27 hours of delivery. The court held that that boat was not of merchantable quality and the purchaser won the case. (Rasbora v JCL Marine (1977) 1 Lloyds Rep. 645)

■ A woman goes into a shoe shop and tries on a pair of shoes. The shoes look all right but they have an unsightly mark on them which the woman fails to notice. Next day the woman wears the shoes and one of the heels drops off. She looks at the shoes again and at this point notices the mark for the first time. She goes back to the shop and complains both about the defective heel and the unsightly mark. The shop would be within their rights to argue that the woman should have noticed the mark when she tried on the shoes and that as she failed to do so she cannot now complain about it. They cannot say the same about the heel as the defect in it was not obvious at the time of purchase. The shoes therefore are unmerchantable and as the woman has come straight back with them she is entitled to her money back and damages.

Fit for the purpose

Section 14(3) of the Sale of Goods Act provides further protection for purchasers. This states that where a trader sells goods and

> ... the buyer expressly or by implication makes known to the seller any particular purpose for which the goods are being bought there is an implied condition that the goods supplied under the contract are reasonably fit for that purpose whether or not that is a purpose for which such goods are commonly supplied, except where the circumstances show that the buyer does not rely, or that it is unreasonable for him to rely on the skill or judgement of the seller.

This means that goods purchased must be reasonably fit for the purpose for which they are required (a) if the buyer tells the seller what the goods are wanted for *or* (b) if it is obvious from the surrounding circumstances what the buyer wants the goods for. In either situation it makes no difference to the seller's obligations under this section if the goods in question are normally utilized for some other purpose.

The buyer is not protected under this section if it is obvious that the buyer placed no reliance on any expertise the seller might have when deciding to make the purchase, or if in the circumstances it would not be reasonable for them to do so. This provision is mostly relevant to commercial transactions where a professional purchaser may well know as much or more than the seller, and would be much harder to prove in the case of a consumer sale.

■ The plaintiff, a draper, went to the shop of the defendant, a retail chemist, and asked for a 'hot-water bottle'. An article was 'shown to him as such' and he then purchased it. Five days later the bottle burst while in use and scalded the person using it. The court held the buyer had 'by implication' made it obvious (i.e. it was clear from the surrounding circumstances) what the hot-water bottle was wanted for and that it was not fit for that purpose. The buyer, being unskilled in the matter of hot-water bottles', had relied on the seller's skill and judgement. The purchaser won the case. (Preist v Last (1903) 2 KB 148, 153)

■ A man goes into a shop to buy something to grind nuts in. He sees a coffee grinder in the shop and asks the assistant if it would be suitable for grinding nuts. He is told that it would be. He buys it but later, when he tries to grind nuts in it, it breaks down. He could claim the protection of Section 14(3). He made it clear what he wanted the grinder for; the fact that it is normally used for grinding coffee beans is irrelevant. He obviously relied on the expertise of the seller.

Secondhand goods

Purchasers of secondhand goods are protected by the two provisions of Section 14 but the fact that the goods are not new would be a factor to be taken into account when considering what standard of quality it would be reasonable to expect. In a case quoted below the judge actually said: 'A buyer should realize that when he buys a secondhand car defects may appear sooner or later . . .' As we have already pointed out, the point at which an article becomes legally not up to standard is difficult to define. Cases regarding secondhand cars illustrate this point.

■ A purchaser bought a secondhand car. He knew when he bought it that the cluch needed some attention and indeed negotiated a lower price on that account. Later he discovered that the clutch would cost more to repair than he had anticipated. He lost the case because the court decided the above complaint was not sufficiently serious for them to find that the car was unmerchantable or unfit for the purpose required. The judge made the comment quoted above. (Bartlett v Sidney Marcus Ltd (1965) 1 WLR 1013)

■ A man who knew nothing about cars inspected and then bought a secondhand Jaguar. The dealer commended its quality and condition and said that despite its mileage of 82,165 it was 'hardly run in'. The purchaser drove 2,354 miles in it over a three-week period, then the engine blew up on the motorway and another had to be put in. The purchaser located the previous owner who had sold the 'hardly run in' car to the dealer. This person interestingly told the court: 'At the time of resale I thought the engine was clapped out. I do not think this engine was fit to be used on a road, not really. It needed a rebore.' The court decided that the seller had breached the provisions of Section 14. The purchaser won the case. (Crowther v Shannon Motor Co. (1975) 1 WLR 30)

Durability

There are no hard and fast rules about how long a product is expected to last. The provisions of Section 14 are concerned only with the state of the product on the day of purchase. However, the fact that a product ceases to function some time after purchase can be used as evidence that at the time it was bought it was not of sufficiently high quality. In the case above, the engine that went for 2,300 miles and then blew up was not up to standard.

Each case would depend on its own particular facts and things like whether the product was new or secondhand, how much was paid for it and what sort of item it was would obviously be relevant. In one court case a judge said that goods should continue to be fit for their purpose 'for a reasonable time after delivery' and 'what is a reasonable time will depend upon the nature of the goods'. (Lord Diplock: Lambert v Lewis (1981) 2 WLR, p. 720)

It is because of the general uncertainty in this area that a consumer with a guarantee may end up with a better deal than someone who has only Sale of Goods Act protection.

Complain quickly

Once you realize there's something wrong with a product purchased then it is important to act quickly if you want the right to get all your money back. A buyer who delays too long may lose the right to a complete refund and will therefore only be able to claim damages. A purchaser who can prove that a seller has done any of the following has the right to a complete refund *and* damages:

- misdescribed the goods (Section 13, Sale of Goods Act).
- sold shoddy goods (Section 14, Sale of Goods Act).
- violated an important contract term (the contract in question can be either verbal or written), i.e. broken a condition (as opposed to a warranty) in England, Wales and Northern Ireland; broken a material term in Scotland (see *Legal explanation*).

The buyer can lose the right to a refund and be left with only the right to damages in the following circumstances:

- England, Wales and Northern Ireland: The purchaser loses the right to a refund by 'accepting' the goods in the legal sense. Acceptance takes place when the buyer either tells the seller she/he has accepted the goods (or signs something to that effect), or does something to the goods which is inconsistent with the seller retaining ownership, e.g. selling the goods to someone else or altering them in some way. Acceptance will be *assumed* if the purchaser keeps the goods for a reasonable lapse of time and fails to tell the seller s/he does not want them. Hence it is important to complain quickly.
- Scotland: The purchaser loses the right to a refund once a reasonable period of time has gone by.

Dangerous goods

Sometimes goods purchased may turn out to be in a dangerous condition. A car might crash on the motorway injuring the driver and passengers. An electric appliance could cause a fire to start in the home which results in considerable damage. A toy bought for a child might shatter during play; even if the child was not injured the parents might want to take some action so that other children are protected.

People injured or suffering economic loss as a result of goods being sold in a dangerous condition have a variety of options open to them and these are all set out below. Both the purchaser of the goods and other people affected may have rights to sue either the seller or the manufacturer for damages, depending on the circumstances. There is also the possibility that either the seller or the manufacturer could be prosecuted in the criminal courts. As explained under *Fine print* (p. 26), traders cannot evade responsibility for injuries caused by dangerous goods, nor for economic loss unless that was considered reasonable.

Rights under the Sale of Goods Act 1979

As explained under *Shoddy goods* (see pp. 29–33), Section 14 of the Sale of Goods Act obliges the trader to supply goods that are both of merchantable quality and fit for the purpose required. Goods sold in a dangerous condition would probably satisfy neither of these conditions and, if so, the purchaser could sue the trader for breach of these conditions if s/he was injured or suffered economic loss because of the dangerous state of the goods when sold. Other people affected would have no rights to sue under the Sale of Goods Act because only the purchaser has made a contract with the trader and this Act covers only the parties to the contract. However, they may be able to obtain redress under other provisions (see below).

The right to sue for negligence

Negligence is the legal term for carelessness. Various court cases have decided the circumstances in which a person injured or suffering loss because of someone else's careless behaviour can sue that person for damages in the civil court. The aggrieved person has to establish:

- That the wrongdoer owed a 'duty of care' to the injured person. Manufacturers of goods and retailers who sell goods owe a duty of care not only to the person who bought the goods but to anyone else who is injured as a result of the use of the goods provided injury to those other people is 'reasonably forseeable'.
- That the wrongdoer has been negligent, i.e. has not been as careful as they ought to have been.
- That as a result of this careless behaviour by the wrongdoer the aggrieved person has been injured or has suffered economic loss.

The law of negligence is not easy to understand and there is not room here to explain it fully. This is one area where you should definitely take advice before considering going to court, particularly if the injuries have been serious.

- A man bought some Golden Fleece underwear. After wearing the garments he contracted dermatitis. He was able to prove that he got the dermatitis because excess sulphites had been carelessly left in the underwear during the process of manufacture. He successfuly sued the manufacturers for negligence. (Grant v Australian Knitting Mills Ltd (1936) AC 85)

- A woman bought some jewellery cleaning fluid at a well-known London store. The fluid was contained in a plastic bottle and when the woman removed the screw cap the plug flew out, the fluid squirted into her eyes and injured her. She sued the store and won the case as the court held the store had been negligent. The court came to this conclusion because they found the store had marketed the fluid without making proper enquiries. The store knew the bottles leaked. The inexperienced manufacturer's response to this phenomenon had been to seal up the hole in the bottle's plug, causing the build-up of pressure inside the bottle. The court also found that the constituents of the fluid were dangerous and there was no warning to this effect on the bottle. The store were negligent because they had not made proper investigations after noticing the bottles leaked and had not ensured an adequate warning was fixed to the bottles. (Note that in this case the consumer sued the retailer and not the manufacturer. If a retailer is affluent and still in business whereas the manufacturer has gone bankrupt there are obvious advantages in suing the former.) (Fisher v Harrods Ltd (1966) 1 Lloyds Rep. 500)

■ A woman went into a cafe with a friend. The friend bought a bottle of ginger beer. The cafe owner poured the woman a glassful and she drank it. The friend then filled her own glass and out floated the decomposed remains of a snail. The woman suffered shock as a result of the nauseating sight and gastroenteritis because of the impurities she had already consumed. The woman sued the manufactures for negligence and won the case. (Note that she was successful even though she didn't buy the ginger beer herself.) (Donoghue v Stevenson (1932) AC 562)

■ The drug Thalidomide was developed in Germany and promoted widely as a safe tranquillizer without side-effects. It was marketed in the UK by the Distillers Co. (Biochemicals) Ltd. A number of children were born deformed as a result of their mothers taking this drug whilst pregnant, and some of them tried to sue Distillers for damages. In order to win the case the children's lawyers would have had to prove that Distillers had been negligent; the bare fact that the drug had caused the injuries was not sufficient. Neither the German company nor Distillers had tested the drug's effects on the developing foetus, although the latter had advertised the drug as being safe for pregnant women and nursing mothers. However, Distillers were able to establish that at the relevant time the potentially damaging effect of drugs on the developing foetus was not appreciated and that tests of this sort were not customary.

Lawyers acting for the children were therefore not confident that they could win the case in court because of the difficulty of establishing fault on the part of Distillers. So the case was settled out of court for sums of money which were criticized as being too low.

Distillers did in fact pay out more later as a result of adverse public opinion, but this case does illustrate the difficulties a consumer might face when trying to win a negligence case. The 'fault' basis of negligence has been criticized. In 1985 an EEC Directive concerning manufacturers' liability for their products was adopted. Our law in this area must therefore be changed within three years of the adoption. People injured or suffering economic loss after using a defective product will be able to sue the producer without having to prove fault, although producers will have certain 'defences' available to them.

Criminal prosecution

There are numerous statutes which specify that selling particular types of unsafe goods is a criminal offence. There are no generalized provisions about this so unless the goods in question are covered by legislation, the person who sold them cannot be prosecuted even if the goods do turn out to be dangerous. However, the government intends to change the law so that all suppliers of goods will be under a duty to ensure that goods they supply conform with sound modern standards of safety.

The consumer protection acts and The Consumer Safety Act 1978 were passed with the object of protecting consumers from the sale of products that could cause injuries. As and when it becomes apparent that a particular product on the market is a potential source of danger, the government can bring in a regulation either banning its sale altogether or banning its sale in that condition. Anyone who disobeys these orders can be prosecuted in the criminal courts. Orders have been made concerning stands for carrycots, nightdresses, electrical appliances, cooking utensils, heating appliances, pencils and graphic instruments, toys, glazed ceramics, children's clothing, babies' dummies, cosmetics, prams and pushchairs, balloon-making compounds, upholstered furniture, expanding novelties, toy watersnakes, scented erasers and pedal bicycles. Examples of such orders are the Upholstered Furniture (Safety) Regulations 1980, which state that upholstered furniture must not be sold unless it has passed the 'smouldering cigarette test' and the Pedal Bicycles (Safety) Regulations 1984 which state that bicycles must be manufactured in accordance with British Standards (see p. 188) or the equivalent. It is not possible here to list all the products covered at the moment and the categories are being expanded all the time. If uncertain whether a product is covered or not, contact your local authority's Trading Standards Department and they should be able to tell you. It is worth doing this even if the goods turn out not to be covered because it is only as a result of consumer complaints that they ever will be.

In emergencies, when it is necessary to act quickly, the government can also issue prohibition orders forbidding the sale of a particular suspected dangerous product and prohibition notices addressed to a particular trader forbidding them to sell particular goods. Notices to warn can also be directed to manufacturers ordering them to publish at their own expense warnings about goods which are considered to be unsafe. If these notices are disobeyed the person to whom they were addressed can be prosecuted.

Legislation also provides for the prosecution of those who alter food so as to make it injurious to health if they have done so with the intention that the food be sold for human consumption in that state. Anyone who sells or offers to sell such food can also be prosecuted, as can those who sell or offer to sell any food which is intended for but is unfit for human consumption. (See p. 18 for relevant legislation.)

■ A family went into a restaurant and lemonade was ordered for the children. They were supplied with caustic soda. Arguments by those responsible that they were not guilty because what was offered was not food did not avail them and they were found guilty. The court said that as the substance provided was something that purported to be food and had been demanded by the purchaser, that was sufficient. (Meah v Roberts 1978 1 AE 97)

The government also has power under the legislation to make regulations (the breach of which would be a criminal offence) with the object of regulating food additives and processing in the interests of public health. Ministers must also 'have regard to the desirability of restricting, so far as practicable, the use of substances of no nutritional value as foods or as ingredients of foods'. Regulations have been made about a wide range of foods, including mustard, self-raising flour, curry powder, tomato ketchup, fish cakes and salad cream. If something you eat makes you ill, it is always worth complaining to your local authority. We do not have space here to go into all the laws about unsafe foods but consumers do have considerable protection in this area.

Other statutes controlling the sale of dangerous goods include the Medicines Act, which makes it an offence to sell adulterated medical products or ones which are not of the nature and quality demanded by the purchaser. Also, the Road Traffic Acts state that it is an offence to sell a motor vehicle in an unroadworthy condition. If a successful prosecution takes place under any statute the consumer may be awarded compensation (see p. 199).

If a trader or manufacturer has breached a legal duty set out in a statute then, apart from any criminal penalty or compensation order they might incur, the aggrieved consumer might in addition be able to sue them in the civil court for damages for breach of that duty. Any such action might well be combined with a claim for breach of the Sale of Goods Act and/or negligence (see above). This, too, is a difficult area of law and one where advice should be taken before embarking on any litigation.

Other problems

No deal

A consumer may decide to purchase something because of an advertisement in a shop window or because s/he has seen something on display on a shelf inside. What if the shopkeeper, despite the advertisement or display, refuses to sell the item at all or demands a different price to that advertised?

Unfortunately, at present, the customer has no right to go to the civil court and insist that traders keep to the bargain they have offered. That is because the courts have decided in various cases that putting notices outside trade premises offering to sell goods at a certain price or displaying goods on the shelves inside is only what lawyers call an 'invitation to treat'. A customer who wants the goods must then 'offer' to buy them and the trader can turn down this offer if s/he wishes (see *Legal explanation*). One leading case on the subject concerned a well-known chain of chemist's accused of selling drugs without proper supervision by a registered pharmacist. The store's pharmacist was standing by the till and the store successfully argued that the contract was only concluded at that point and not when a customer selected an item at an advertised price from the shelves.*

A demand by a trader that a consumer pay more for the goods than the price advertised or else do without them could, however, amount to a criminal offence. Section 11(2) of the Trade Descriptions Act states: 'If a person offering to supply goods gives, by whatever means, any indication likely to be taken as an indication that the goods are being offered at a price less than that at which they are in fact being offered . . .' then that person is guilty of an offence. It is always worth reporting a trader to your local authority if you are misled by an advertisement in this way.

A customer could also take action if it could be proved that the refusal to do business was based on racial or sexual discrimination. The Race Relations Act 1976 and the Sex Discrimination Act 1975 state that it is unlawful for someone selling goods to discriminate against a customer on grounds of race or sex. The Acts do not apply in Northern Ireland but the Sex Discrimination (Northern Ireland) Order 1976 makes similar provision in respect of sex discrimination. Traders who refuse to provide goods of the same quality, in the same manner and on the same terms as they normally do to other customers are in breach of these Acts and could be taken to the civil courts and forced to pay damages to the aggrieved customer. The consumer could take the trader to court him/herself or report what has happened to the Commission for Racial Equality (Elliott J. House, Allington Street, London SW1. Tel: 01-828 7022) or the Equal Opportunities Commission (Overseas House, Quay Street, Manchester 3. Tel: 061-833 9244 and offices in Scotland and Northern Ireland). Either of these bodies could assist with the court case.

No goods

Customers who buy goods may make an arrangement with the seller that the goods be delivered later to their home addresss. There may be no specific agreement as to when this is to take place or a precise time may have been agreed and it may be vital to the consumer that the goods do not arrive late.

Customers who want the goods delivered before or on a specific date *must* make this clear to the seller. It is best to do so in writing;

---

* Pharmaceutical Society of Great Britain v Boots (1953) 1 QB 401.

that way it is easier to prove the existence of the agreement. The legal phrase to use is 'time is of the essence', i.e. time is vital. It is also worth specifying, preferably in writing, why time is so vital. If you do both these things then you will have more rights against the trader if the goods do not arrive. If there's no agreement then the goods must be delivered within a reasonable time. This is stated in Section 29(3) of the Sale of Goods Act. What is reasonable would depend on all the circumstances. Also, the goods must be delivered at a reasonable hour.

If the goods do not arrive by the agreed date and it has been stated that time is of the essence, the purchaser can refuse to accept the goods at a later time and claim a refund where applicable. In any other situation you should write to the shop giving them one final chance and time limit in which to deliver and make it clear that you will not be prepared to accept the goods and, where applicable, that you will demand a refund if they are brought after that time. In all cases, if the goods never arrive or arrive late the customer is entitled to damages. If the trader was made aware of the implications of late delivery then those losses can be claimed for as well, hence the importance of making sure they know what non-delivery would mean to you.

As stated under *Fine print* on p. 26, attempts by traders to avoid performing their side of the contract are of no effect unless reasonable.

Safety in the shop

Sometimes a customer may have an accident whilst in a shop. For example, something might fall off a shelf and hit someone on the head or an elderly person might slip on a greasy floor and break a limb.

The Occupier's Liability Acts (1957 England and Northern Ireland; 1960 Scotland) impose on shopkeepers a duty to ensure that members of the public will be reasonably safe whilst on their premises. Thus if an accident occurs which is their fault they could be sued by consumers for breach of their duty under the Occupier's Liability Acts. Shop owners must be prepared for the fact that children are likely to be less careful than adults. Shopkeepers cannot use an exclusion clause to evade their responsibilities for injuries caused by an accident in the shop. If there is a claim for damage to property then the exclusion clause could only be relied on if it was reasonable.

Trading associations

Some retailers are members of trading associations and if a customer is dissatisfied with such a retailer then they can consider complaining to the trading association concerned as well as or instead of pursuing their legal rights. The trading associations publish codes of practice and their members are supposed to stick to the rules that are contained in those codes. The codes do *not* have the force of law and can only supplement or add to the legal rights which the customer already has. There are codes at present in relation to the sale of cars, motorcycles, furniture, footwear and electrical goods but new categories of goods may be covered in the future.

Below we set out some of the most useful features of the codes, particularly those that give you more rights than you have under the law.

Cars and motorcycles

There are three trading associations concerning cars, all of which subscribe to the same code of practice. A garage might belong to any one of them and if so should display the relevant symbol. They are the Motor Agents Association (MAA), the Society of Motor Manufacturers and Traders (SMMT) (the only one to which manufacturers belong) and the Scottish Motor Trade Association (SMTA). Their code includes the following provisions:

- New cars 'must be delivered in condition which is to the manufacturer's standard' and, where the dealer is required by the manufacturer to carry out a pre-delivery inspection, a copy of the PDI checklist must be given to the customer. Order forms must specify *all* charges additional to the car price and the customer must be given a copy of the manufacturer's handbook.
- Manufacturers' guarantees must be in terms which are 'easily understandable' and the customer should be told of these terms. The unexpired period of a guarantee should be transferable to subsequent owners and manufacturers should be prepared to extend the guarantee period if the car has been off the road for an extended period.
- With used cars, dealers should carry out a pre-sales inspection, list all defects discovered and give a copy of this checklist to the customer. Copies of relevant written

information available from previous owners (e.g. service records) must be passed on to the customer. Dealers must attempt to verify the recorded mileage and if they cannot do so the customer must be informed. If a written guarantee is not used then 'any specific promises which the dealer is willing to make in relation to used cars should be set out in writing'. Advertisements and descriptions regarding used cars must not contain terms which 'are likely to be misunderstood by the customer or which are not capable of exact definition'. For example, if the word 'reconditioned' is used, the nature of the reconditioning must be carefully explained.

● All advertisements regarding cars must comply with the ASA and IBA codes of practice (see p. 22).
● Complaints should be made first to the garage and then, if relating to a guarantee on a new car, to the manufacturer.

Thereafter the customer may omplain to whichever trading association the garage belongs, or to the SMMT if the complaint relates to a manufacturers guarantee. The addresses are:

● The Customer Relations Department, SMMT, Forbes House, Halkin Street, London SW1X 7DS.
● The Conciliation Service, MAA, 73 Park Street, Bristol BSI 5PS. and MAA, 107a Shore Road, Belfast 15.
● The Customer Complaints Service, SMTA, 3 Palmerston Place, Edinburgh EH12 5AQ.

If the trading association do not resolve the matter you can, on paying a fee (which might be refunded if you win), agree to go to arbitration instead of going to court. Take legal advice before deciding which to opt for. *You cannot do both*.

There is now also a code of practice for motorcycles with similar provisions. Four motorcycle trade associations subscribe to this code. They are:

● The Motor Cycle Association, Starley House, Eaton Road, Coventry CV1 2FH (for complaints about new bikes).
● The Motor Agents Association, 73 Park Street, Bristol BS1 5PS.
● The Motorcycle Retailers Association, 31A High Street, Tunbridge Wells, Kent TN1 1XN.
● The Scottish Motor Trade Association, 3 Palmerston Place, Edinburgh EH12 5AQ.

(The last three deal with complaints against member dealers.)

Furniture

Some retailers and manufacturers have joined either the National Association of Retail Furnishers, 17–21 George Street, Croydon CR9 1QT or the Scottish House Furnishers Association, 203 Pitt Street, Glasgow G2 4DB. Both these associations have agreed to be bound by the same code of practice which covers the sale of new household furniture (including carpets). Members agree to be bound by the ASA and IBA Codes of Advertising (see p. 22) and also the Furniture Code Glossary. The latter gives directions about the proper use of descriptive terms. For example, if something is described as being of 'solid wood' it must not contain plywood, hardboard or chipboard.

If a customer is dissatisfied and a complaint to the retailer does not resolve matters the complaint can then be referred to the relevant trading association. The association may send an independant examiner to inspect the goods and this will presently cost the customer £14 (refundable if the complaint is substantiated). If this does not resolve matters, the customer can agree to go to arbitration instead of to court. The customer will be charged a fee for the arbitration (refundable if they win). Take legal advice before deciding whether to agree to arbitration or to go to court. *You cannot do both.*

Footwear

Some retailers and manufacturers of footwear have joined the Footwear Distributors' Federation (FDF), Commonwealth House, 1–19 New Oxford Street, London WC1 1PA. Tel: 01-404 0955. The FDF has produced a code of practice and retailer members must display the symbol and have a copy of the code in their shops available for inspection by customers. Retailers who consistently offend against the code of practice can be excluded from the scheme. The code states that:

- All advertisements, window displays, etc. must give clear and accurate information regarding the products offered and members agree to be bound by the ASA and IBA Codes of Advertising (see p. 22).

- Children's feet should always be measured to avoid risk of damage.
- If a customer has a complaint and the shop does not settle the matter (the code says justifiable complaints *should* be settled immediately), the retailer can offer to send the shoes back to the suppliers for an expert opinion free of charges. Alternatively, if the customer requests it, the shoes can be sent to the Footwear Testing Centre for examination. The customer will have to pay a contribution (currently £3.70) towards the test fee but this will be refunded if the Centre finds in the customer's favour. The supervising board of the Centre does include a consumer representative amongst its members. The Centre's report should be ready in three days and members agree to be bound by all findings favourable to the customer. If that does not resolve matters, or at any other time, the customer can go to court.

Electrical goods

Some retailers of electrical goods have joined the Radio, Electrical and Television Retailers Association (RETRA), 100 St Martins Lane, London WC2N 4BD. Tel: 01-836 1463/4/5/6. Their code of practice states that:

- Advertising must be clear and honest and comply with the ASA and IBA codes (see p. 22).
- Members must guarantee new goods for a minimum of 12 months for parts and labour. If, during the guarantee period, faults cannot be rectified within 15 working days, the dealer must endeavour to lend the same or a similar item to the customer.
- If a member retailer will not resolve a complaint satisfactorily then the customer can refer it to the secretary of RETRA. If that fails to resolve the matter, it can be referred on to the RETRA conciliation panel, which does include a consumer representative. The decision should be available within 15 days and members must honour it. The customer can still and at any time go to court.

2.

Outside buying

Buying goods at home

Doorstep salesperson

Most people have at least once encountered a doorstep salesperson. Whatever is being offered may turn out to be a good bargain and the seller may have a pleasant approach. Conversely the item sold may turn out to be a very bad bargain indeed or the seller may prove to be offensive and difficult to get rid of.

In the previous chapters we described the rights of a customer buying goods in trade premises. The buyer has exactly the same rights of redress against doorstep sellers *and any company they are employed by*.

In addition, anyone selling goods commits a criminal offence if whilst calling from house to house (or via the post or telephone) they imply falsely to a potential customer that blind or disabled persons are employed in the production, preparation or packaging of those goods or would benefit from the sale of them. This is stated in the Trading Representations (Disabled Persons) Acts 1958 and 1972 (Northern Ireland is covered by a separate Act.) Local authorities, firms who genuinely do employ large numbers of disabled people and disabled people who are selling goods they made themselves are excepted from this rule. If anyone else makes such claims you could report him/her to your local authority who might prosecute.

If a doorstep seller refuses to leave your home when asked then they have committed a trespass. This is not a criminal offence (except in certain limited circumstances not applicable here) but trespassers can be sued in the civil court for damages. The home owner can use reasonable force (i.e. the least necessary) to eject a trespasser and if the seller really will not leave the police are sometimes prepared to assist in the removal of trespassers.

Practical hints

The above sets out the legal position but there are some practical hints which should be noted:

- Is the person really selling something? S/he might say so but in fact might want to get into your house for some other nefarious purpose. Never let anyone into your home without seeing an identity card first, and it's probably wise never to let them in if there are two of them and one of you. *If in doubt, keep them on the doorstep.*
- Conversely, someone who, for example, says s/he would like to interview you for the purposes of market research, may actually want to sell you something instead. Once you know this your attitude to him/her may change. Don't be afraid to tell such people to leave; you can end their permission to be in your home or on your doorstep at any time. They then become trespassers.

Which doorstep sellers are safe to do business with?

All the legal rights in the world won't help a buyer who has purchased something from a doorstep seller if the latter gives a false name and address and then vanishes from the area never to be seen again. If the item bought did not cost much it is not the end of the world but someone planning to buy an expensive product from a doorstep seller ought to be particularly careful. In such circumstances it is vital to ensure that you know who to sue when things go wrong and where to find them.

Some firms who employ doorstep sellers are members of a trading association called the Direct Selling Association (DSA 44 Russell Square, London WC1B 4JP. Tel: 01-580 8433). Members of the DSA have voluntarily agreed to be bound by the DSA's code of practice. (Remember that codes of practice do not have the force of law and can only complement or add to any legal rights the purchaser already has. The code states under the heading 'Identification' that 'All direct salespersons should immediately identify themselves to the prospective customer. They should also indicate the purpose of their approach to the customer and identify the direct seller or manufacturer with whom they are associated and the product line with which they deal.' Later under this heading it is stated: 'Copies of this code of practice should be available for perusal by customers.' Members of the DSA must give customers a written guarantee of the quality of their products and customers are to have a minimum of 14 days in which to cancel any order. Anyone who wishes to complain about the behaviour of a doorstep seller from a member company should firstly complain to that company – the seller has a duty under the code to tell you the name of the company. If that does not resolve the matter, the complaint can be referred on to the DSA itself, and if that fails the code administrator will arbitrate (see p. 196). If the administrator decides the member has breached the code, the member can be ordered to give the customer a refund or repair or replace the product in question. The customer does not have to pay for the arbitration and is not precluded by it from taking the case to court. At the moment about 33 companies belong to the DSA, including Avon Cosmetics, Encyclopaedia Britannica, Linguaphone and Tupperware.

If you are confronted by doorstep sellers who do not belong to the DSA and you still want to do business with them, then at the very least demand to know which organization they claim to represent. If you have no personal knowledge of the organization concerned and you're thinking of spending a lot of money then it is worth checking that it does exist and that the doorstep seller does indeed work for it. If the seller is a sole trader and the product is expensive then you are certainly taking a risk if you buy it.

Remember, you can report any doorstep sellers to your local authority or the Office of Fair Trading if you think they have behaved badly and that something should be done about it.

Buying by post

Mail order

A large amount of goods are bought by post. Customers may order through a catalogue or respond to an advertisement in a newspaper or magazine. Problems may arise when money is sent and no goods arrive or the wrong or damaged goods are received. Sometimes goods are sent which the customer has not ordered at all.

A customer who buys goods through the post has the same rights of redress against the mail order seller as the customer buying goods in trade premises.

In addition, any persons who place an advertisement or distribute a circular or catalogue offering goods for sale by post and requesting money in advance must state in the advertisement their true name, registered business name and the address at which the business is managed. If they do not do so they commit a criminal offence and can be prosecuted under Section 23 of the Fair Trading Act 1973. This is stated in the Mail Order Transactions (Information) Order 1976, the object of which was to provide some protection for consumers against crooked traders advertising an article in a newspaper, requesting payment in advance and then making off with all the money sent in without, of course, sending any goods in return.

Sales on approval and sale or return

A sale on approval is one where goods are delivered to a buyer and the buyer is allowed to inspect the goods and try them out before deciding whether to purchase them or not. If you order goods on this basis take great care to read the approval agreement or you may find yourself stuck with something you don't want.

Section 18, Rule 4 of the Sale of Goods Act sets out at what point goods delivered on approval are considered to become the buyer's property. This is important because once ownership of the goods passes from seller to buyer the buyer must pay for the goods whether s/he wants them or not, even if something adverse happens to them, e.g. they get stolen. Goods become buyers' property if:

- Buyers signify to the seller that they want to keep the goods.
- Buyers do something which makes it clear they regard the goods as theirs. Selling them to somebody else would be an obvious example of this. Using them excessively might be sufficient too.
- The approval time set out in the agreement has expired. Hence the importance of reading what is in the agreement. It is also important to keep a copy of any communication sent to the seller in which you have said you don't want the goods.
- There is no agreement and a reasonable amount of time has elapsed.

Whilst the goods remain the property of the seller buyers must still take reasonable care of them and if they do not do so they might have to reimburse the seller for any damage caused.

If goods are supplied on a 'sale or return' basis the buyer is allowed to return to the seller that part of the goods which the buyer does not want. For example, if you receive 100 cans of beer on a sale or return basis prior to giving a party, you can return those which the guests did not drink and get your money back. However, the same rules apply as above, so if you do not return the excess unwanted goods within the time agreed or within a reasonable time you will not be able to get your money back and will have to keep the goods.

Damage in transit

The seller has a duty to pack the goods in such a way that they can last out a normal journey and be of merchantable quality and fit for their purpose on arrival. This has been decided in various court cases. If the goods are damaged as a result of faulty packaging, the buyer can demand redress from the seller. The seller must also make reasonable arrangements for the transport of the goods. For example, sending something perishable like clotted cream by an obviously slow route would not be acceptable. This principle is stated in Section 32(2) of the Sale of Goods Act.

Apart from these duties the seller may not be held legally responsible if the goods get damaged on the way. However, the buyer might be able to sue the transporter of the goods if what happened was their fault. Legally this is not of much use where the carrier is the post office because of the considerable amount of immunity which that organization enjoys, although a consumer might be voluntarily compensated under the GPO's code of practice (see p. 107).

Unsolicited goods

At one time it was common for unscrupulous traders to send unasked-for goods to consumers and then bully the latter for payment. This activity has been greatly curtailed by the Unsolicited Goods and Services Act 1971. (In Northern Ireland refer to the Unsolicited Goods and Services (Northern Ireland) Order 1976.) Section 1 of the Act states that anyone receiving unsolicited goods can keep them without having to pay for them once a period of 6 months has gone by and the seller has not called to collect them. Consumers can shorten this procedure by writing to the seller stating their name and address, the fact that the goods were unsolicited and, if applicable, specifying any alternative address from which the goods can be collected. The consumer may then keep the goods if the seller does not take them away within 30 days. The recipient must not, however, unreasonably refuse to let the seller take the goods away within the 6-month or 30-day period.

Section 2 of the same Act prevents sellers from trying to bully consumers into paying for goods that were not requested in the first place. It is a criminal offence to demand payment for unsolicited goods, to threaten to take legal proceedings, to place or threaten to place someone's name on a list of defaulters or debtors, or threaten or use other collection procedures (e.g. debt collection agencies), if unsolicited goods are not paid for. The Unsolicited Goods and Services (Invoices, etc.) Regulations 1975 further provide that sellers of unsolicited goods who want legally to mention a price must print their invoice on white paper using black or dark grey letters. In large red letters on every page must be printed the words: THIS IS NOT A DEMAND FOR PAYMENT. THERE IS NO OBLIGATION TO PAY. THIS IS NOT A BILL.

The effect of these provisions is that traders who try and demand payment for unsolicited goods by any method other than the approved one mentioned above can be prosecuted. Traders may be acquitted if they can establish that they had a reasonable cause to believe they had a right to payment. A well-known seller of magazines used this defence when their computer wrongly sent out a demand for payment because it had not be reprogrammed as it should have been. They were, surprisingly, found not guilty. (Readers Digest Association v Pirie 1973 SLT 170)

Section 4 of the same Act provides that it is also a criminal offence to send a book, magazine or leaflet which the seller knows is unsolicited and which describes or illustrates human sexual techniques. Someone who is offended by the receipt of unrequested pornography can therefore report the person who sent it to their local authority who might prosecute.

Non-legal protection

The ASA and IBA codes of advertising (see p. 22) both have sections about mail order advertisements. Section CV 19 of the ASA code covers advertisements where consumers are requested to send money in advance. It states that this money must be returned together with a refund for the costs of returning the item where applicable in the following circumstances:

1. If unwanted goods are returned undamaged within 7 days by the consumer. Note that later the code says the advertiser need

not accept responsibility for returned goods if the consumer has no proof of postage, so make sure you get this from the Post Office. The code also says later that it will be assumed that the consumer can try goods out (as long as the goods are not damaged in the process) unless the advertiser specifically forbids this.

2. If there is a money-back guarantee (however expressed).
3. If the goods sent do not correspond with the description in the advertisement.
4. If consumers state that they want their money back because of the delay that has taken place. Later the code says that in most circumstances (plants are not included) goods should be delivered within 28 days.
5. If the advertiser is in breach of contract for any other reason, e.g. shoddy goods.

The IBA insist on an undertaking from advertisers that full refunds will be given to customers who are justifiably dissatisfied with the product or who have suffered delay in receiving it.

In addition, some mail order traders have joined trading associations and have therefore voluntarily agreed to be bound by the code of practice put out by those associations. If the code is breached by a member firm consumers can complain to the trading association concerned if the trader is not prepared to put the matter right. If that does not resolve the problem the code might provide for further consideration of the consumer's complaint (see below). Do not forget, codes of practice do not have the force of law and consumers still have all the legal rights already listed.

Catalogue sales

Some catalogue mail order companies are members of the Mail Order Traders Association, 25 Castle Street, Liverpool L2 4TD. Tel: 051-236 7581. This association publishes a code of practice which lists member firms and these firms must also state the fact of their membership in their mail order catalogues. Under the code members have a number of obligations. These include compliance with ASA and IBA codes on advertising (see p. 22) and there is a duty to state clearly the price of goods offered and whether items such as postage are included. Catalogues must also give 'full and clear information' about the goods offered, particularly in relation to size, colour, materials used and important restrictions on use. If goods are damaged in transit then members will replace the item or, if a replacement is not available, refund the customer's money.

Customers must be given a minimum 14-day period within which the goods can be returned and a full refund given. If a quoted delivery date is not kept to then customers can cancel the order and receive a refund. The address to which consumers should send any initial complaint must be stated in the catalogue and if a further complaint to the association does not resolve matters the customer has a choice between going to court or agreeing to arbitration (see p. 196). Do not make this decision before receiving legal advice. *You cannot do both.*

Books, records, cassettes

Some traders who sell books, records and cassettes by post have joined the Mail Order Publishers Authority, 1 New Burlington Street, London W1X 1FD. Tel: 01-437 0706. They publish a code of practice and a list of their members. Their symbol should be used by members in all their advertisements. (A sanction against errant members is withdrawal of the right to use the symbol.) Members are bound by the ASA code of advertising and must when advertising, 'express himself clearly and without ambiguity so that the reader should know exactly what he is being offered and to what he is committing himself by replaying to the advertisement'. There are rules about open-ended commitments to receive a continuing series of goods. These commitments cannot last for more than one year if the buyer wishes to opt out. If the price has gone up to a level the buyer could not reasonably have anticipated then the buyer is allowed to cancel before the year is up. If a supply of 'main choice' books or records is offered consumers must be fully aware of what they are letting themselves in for: they must be given advance notice of the 'main choice' and the means to choose something else. Approval periods must be honoured and if delivery is unduly delayed a customer who wants to cancel and get a refund must be given one. There are other provisions but there is not room to list them all here. If a complaint to the member does not resolve the matter the customer may write to the director of the association. If you complaint is considered unjustified, the director will then advise you of your right to go to court about it.

Newspaper advertisements

If traders who advertise in newspapers go bankrupt after receiving a consumer's money but before sending out any goods then the consumer is left without any legal redress. You cannot sue people for money if they do not have any. Some newspapers have voluntary schemes to compensate consumers who have lost money as a result of such a situation. The well-known national daily and

Sunday newspapers belong to the Mail Order Protection Scheme and there are similar schemes operated by the Periodical Publishers Association, Newspaper Society and the Scottish Newspapers. Mail Order advertisers are vetted before being allowed to place an advertisement and must comply with the provisions of the ASA code (see p. 22). Not all goods are covered, e.g. plants and products appealing to fear or superstition. If you have lost money as a result of responding to a newspaper or periodical advertisement then write to the advertisement manager of the paper concerned. You will probably have to produce the original of the advertisement and proof of payment, and there may be a time limit (three months in the case of national newspapers) so do not delay.

3.

Other ways of buying goods

Auctions

Auctions may be good fun to attend but if intending to buy something expensive there you should be particularly careful as you will not be as well protected as when buying in trade premises. Legally auctioneers are regarded as agents of sellers and their respective liability is a difficult area of law, so if you do consider taking court proceedings yourself you should get legal advice first about who to sue.

Purchasers buying goods at an auction have the same rights as those buying goods at trade premises, with one important exception: where goods are being sold at an auction then the auctioneer and seller *are* permitted to disclaim responsibility for a breach of Section 13 or Section 14 of the Sale of Goods Act and for other breaches of contract. The disclaimer would only be allowed to operate if a court considered it to be reasonable. (See page 28 for what reasonable means in this context.) This means that if you see a notice on the wall in an auction room or a sentence in the auction catalogue saying something like, 'All warranties are excluded', you must be particularly careful to inspect goods before you buy them as you may have no redress if the goods later turn out to be faulty.

Under *No deal* (p. 39) we explained that customers buying in shops generally have no right to insist that shopowners sell them items displayed on the shelves. This is because displaying the items is only an 'invitation to treat'. A similar general rule applies at auctions. The auctioneer does not have to accept any bid made from the floor and bids can be withdrawn. If the sale has been advertised as being without reserve (i.e. there is no minimum price below which the goods will not be sold) and yours is the highest bid you might feel justifiably aggrieved if the auctioneer still will not sell the item to you. It has been suggested that in such a situation you could sue for the right to buy the item at the price you bid, but this is somewhat speculative so you should take legal advice before starting any litigation. Once the hammer has fallen, however, the goods are yours and you must pay for them. This is stated in Section 57 of the Sale of Goods Act.

■ A woman is bidding at an auction. She shouts out a price, no one bids after her and suddenly she decides she no longer wants the item. She shouts, 'I've changed my mind. I don't want it.' As long as she has done this before the hammer falls she is not liable to pay.

Anyone suffering an accident whilst attending an auction might be able to sue the auctioneer under the Occupier's Liability Acts (see p. 41).

Bidding by sellers

The person who owns the goods being sold by the auctioneer obviously has a vested interest in the price being as high as possible and might therefore be tempted to bid him/herself so as to force the price upwards. Section 57(4) of the Sale of Goods Act states that it is not lawful for sellers to bid for their own property *unless* they first notify purchasers that they might do so. The same applies if sellers employ someone else to do the bidding for them. If the seller disobeys this rule the buyer may treat the sale as fraudulent and thus get his/her money back plus damages.

Mock auctions

What are known as 'mock auctions' do not normally take place in auction rooms but more usually occur in the street. Mock auctions are bogus auctions where fast-talking salespersons create an atmosphere of excitement and competitiveness and thereby manage to relieve a large number of people of a large amount of money. The Mock Auctions Act (not applicable in Northern Ireland) is an attempt to outlaw such sales. The Act states that it is an offence to hold a mock auction and a mock auction is stated to occur when goods are sold at a price which is lower than the highest bid, or where the right to bid is restricted to those customers who have already bought or agreed to buy something, or where goods are given away or offered as gifts. A number of sellers have been prosecuted under this Act.

You as the seller

If you are the person whose property is being sold by the auctioneer then you should note that under the Auctions (Bidding Agreements) Acts 1927 and 1969 (not applicable in Northern Ireland) it is a criminal offence to pay a person not to bid at an auction. Persons convicted of this offence can be banned from attending auctions for period. The seller does not have to go through with the sale in such circumstances even if the hammer has fallen. It follows from this that it is not illegal for prospective buyers to form 'rings', i.e. to agree not to bid against each other, if no money changes hands over it. But Section 3 of the 1969 Act provides that if one of the ring is a dealer then the seller does not have to go through with the sale even if the hammer has fallen.

These provisions are of course designed to protect the seller from being cheated by a conspiracy of purchasers who aim to make sure the goods are sold to them at rock bottom prices.

■ In July 1981 nine antique dealers were found guilty at Swansea Crown Court of the offence mentioned above. They had agreed not to bid against each other at an auction and later they held their own private auction. They put money representing the difference between the price they paid at the outside auction and the price paid at the private auction into a kitty which they later shared out amongst themselves. Unfortunately for them, these interesting proceedings were video-recorded. On being found guilty they were fined £500 each and banned from attending auctions for six months. (Reported in Sweet & Maxwell, *Consumer Law Encyclopedia* 1–310)

Buying goods from private individuals

Consumers buying goods from private individuals must be particularly wary as the degree of legal protection available in such a situation is considerably less than that afforded to people buying goods from traders. Sometimes traders pretend to be private individuals so as to evade their legal responsibilities to consumers and there are some legal controls aimed at preventing this sort of behaviour. If a private person sells you something s/he does not own him/herself then you could be in a particularly difficult position, which is why we will deal here with the problems faced by a purchaser who buys something which the seller had no right to sell.

The difference in your rights

- The provisions of Section 14 of the Sale of Goods Act (see *Shoddy goods*, pp. 29–33) which states that goods sold must be of merchantable quality and fit for the purpose required do *not* apply to private sales. The law leaves it to you to make sure you are not buying shoddy goods from a private seller.
- In *Fine print* (pp. 26–9) we dealt with the use of exclusion clauses. The Unfair Contract Terms Act does not apply in the main to people selling privately. This means private sellers can, in some circumstances, validly disclaim responsibility for purchaser dissatisfaction *but* disclaimers for breach of Section 12 (right to sell, see later) and Section 13 (misdescription) and misrepresentation will only be of effect if considered reasonable. (See p. 28 for the meaning of reasonable in this context.)
- We have also described on p. 17 and 37 how prosecutions can take place where goods have been wrongly described or have been sold in a dangerous condition. Private sellers cannot be prosecuted under the Trade Descriptions Act* or the Consumer Safety legislation (but they *can* be prosecuted for selling a vehicle in a dangerous condition).

Your rights

A purchaser who has bought something from a private seller and is dissatisfied may be able to:

- sue for misrepresentation or breach of contract if the seller says or puts into writing something untrue or inaccurate about the goods;
- sue for breach of Section 13 of the Sale of Goods Act if the goods have been misdescribed;
- sue for negligence if the goods turn out to be in a dangerous state. However, providing the necessary degree of carelessness will be much more difficult where private sellers are concerned as they will not normally be expected to possess the same degree of expertise as a trader.

---

*One exception to this arises when a private seller sells something falsely described to a business person who in turn sells the object with the false trade description to a customer. The private person could in such circumstances be prosecuted.

■ A private motorist advertised his car for sale as follows: 'Herald convertible, white, 1961, twin carbs.' The seller did not know this but actually the car consisted of the rear half of a 1961 Herald and the front half of an earlier model. The court decided that the seller was in breach of contract. It was a term of the contract that the car was a 1961 Herald. (Beale v Taylor 1967 3AE 253)

Traders masquerading as individuals

A practice once favoured by traders wishing to evade their legal responsibilities was to advertise something for sale and frame the advertisement to make it appear that a private individual was selling the item. The sale of secondhand cars was a particularly vulnerable area of such activities. Now the Business Advertisements (Disclosure) Order 1977 provides that it is a criminal offence for a trader to advertise an item for sale without making it clear that s/he is a trader, as opposed to a private individual. (This Order does not apply to sale by auction.)

■ A trader placed an advertisement in *Exchange and Mart* for caravanettes but did not disclose he was a trader. He was fined in the Magistrates Court. (Reported in *Consumer Law Encyclopedia*, 2–398/1)

The seller with no right to sell

The person who sells goods may not actually have the legal right to do so. This could be because they or someone else stole the goods or because the goods are subject to a hire purchase agreement and still technically belong to the HP company (see Chapter 9) or for a variety of other reasons.

Under Section 12 of the Sale of Goods Act anyone who sells goods is presumed to have the right to do so. This means that if any person sells goods and the goods are later taken away from the purchaser because another person has a better right to them (see below) then the purchaser is legally entitled to a refund from the seller. This is all very well if you have purchased something from a shop but if the seller is a private person then s/he may well have disappeared, particularly if s/he knew, for example, that the goods were stolen. This is why it is very important when buying from private purchasers to make sure they do genuinely own what they are selling.

If you know or have any suspicion that the goods being offered to you are stolen then you could be prosecuted for the criminal offence of 'handling stolen goods' if you buy them. This applies whoever you buy the goods from. Suspicion that the goods might be stolen can also restrict your rights to retain them. (See below.)

When can the original owner recover the goods from the buyer? The general rule is that sellers cannot pass on to buyers a better right to keep the goods than they had themselves. This is now stated in Section 21 of the Sale of Goods Act which puts into statutory form the time honoured legal maxim, *Nemo dat quod non habet* ('You can't give what you don't have'). An innocent purchaser of stolen goods can therefore be legally forced to return the goods to the person from whom they were stolen without receiving any payment from that person. There are some exceptions to this rather harsh rule. For example:

1. Section 22(1) of the Sale of Goods Act provides that a person who buys goods in an open market in England during normal daylight trading hours without any knowledge that the seller had no rights to sell the goods may keep them no matter what.
2. The Hire Purchase Act 1964 and the Hire Purchase Act (Northern Ireland) 1966 provide that if a private purchaser buys a motor vehicle in ignorance of the fact that it is still subject to a hire purchase agreement or conditional sale agreement then s/he can keep it no matter what.

   There are other exceptions but this is a complicated area of law so it is best to take advice if you find yourself in this situation.

Part II
Buying Services

We all have to pay other people to do things for us occasionally. When the person employed or consulted performs the service badly, gives the wrong advice or charges too much it can be difficult to know how to deal with the situation. This section describes what legal rights of redress a consumer has when paying someone to do a service with or without the inclusion of payments for goods as well. As when buying goods, a consumer may have the right to sue the service person in the civil courts or complain about them, or the service person might be liable to prosecution in the criminal courts.

Consumers' rights when paying for services by credit are detailed in Part III.

4.

The general position

Sales talk

Just as purchasers of goods can be misled by sales talk, people who are intending to pay for a service can also be talked into making an agreement they may later regret. People might claim to be fully qualified trades or professional persons when in fact they are not. They might make false claims about the price they intend to charge or the length of time the job will take. Lies might also be told about the qualities of the goods supplied with the service.

This section deals with verbal agreements to purchase services. The first point to be made is that in fact nothing *should* be agreed verbally. When arranging to have service done it is always better to put everything in writing, particularly the price and the time by which the job should be finished. This makes it far easier to prove what was agreed. In the event of there being nothing in writing the following rights may be available to a consumer misled by sales talk.

Misrepresentation

Consumers have some legal rights when lured into making an agreement to pay for services on the basis of a statement that later turns out to be untrue or incorrect. Such statements are called 'misrepresentations' by lawyers and on p. 15 we have already explained which sorts of misrepresentations consumers can take action about when buying goods.

If a service person makes a misrepresentation about goods supplied with the service then the position is the same as if only goods were being bought. If something untrue or inaccurate is said about the service itself then the same rules also apply. The remedies are the same as well, but if the service person has started on the job the consumer may well have to settle for damages only.

Criminal prosecution

Traders who make false statements about services can be prosecuted in the criminal courts under the Trade Description Act 1968. If such a prosecution were to be successful the aggrieved consumer might be awarded compensation (see p. 199).

Section 14 of the Act states that it is a criminal offence for any trader deliberately or recklessly to make a false statement about the following:

(i) the provision in the course of any trade or business of any services, accommodation or facilities. [Later the section provides that where the 'services' involve the 'application of any treatment or process or the carrying out of any repair' then false statements about the effect of same are included.]

(ii) the nature of any services, accommodation or facilities provided in the course of any trade or business.

(iii) the time at which, manner in which or persons by whom any services, accommodation or facilities are so provided.

(iv) the examination, approval or evaluation by any person of any services, accommodation or facilities so provided or

(v) the location or amenities of any accommodation so provided.

Section 13 of the Act provides that it is an offence falsely to state that the services are provided to any person, e.g. statements of the 'hairdressers to Joan Collins' variety are criminal if untrue.

■ The defendant, a builder and roofer, stood by whilst his partner discussed with a customer the prosposed repair of the customer's roof by a special process known as 'tunerizing'. Later the partner and another man did the repairs and signed a receipt saying this particular process had been used when in fact it had not been. Both partners were found guilty of offences under the Trade Descriptions Act. (Parsons v Barnes (1973) CLR 537)

Traders have the same 'defences' available to them as when being prosecuted for falsely describing goods (see p. 18).

Sales pressure

Consumers talked into paying for a service they later decide they did not want have no remedy on that basis alone. Someone under 18, mentally ill or drunk at the time the agreement was made might be able to get out of it if the service was not a necessary one for them to have (see *Legal explanation* for more details).

Misdescribed service goods

If goods which have been supplied together with a service do not correspond with any description given, the Supply of Goods and Services Act 1982 (which does not apply in Scotland) gives the consumer exactly the same protection as if only goods were being bought. This is stated in Section 3 of the Act which is phrased in the same way as Section 13 of the Sale of Goods Act 1979. The rules are therefore the same (see p. 16 for details).

If goods are misdescribed in Scotland aggrieved consumers would have to claim under Scottish common law or possibly the Sale of Goods Act.

Sales print

This section deals with the effect of the written word on any agreement made by a consumer to purchase services.

Brochures and advertisements

If a service is advertised or described in a newspaper or brochure by the service person and the information given therein is untrue or incorrect then an aggrieved consumer may be able to sue the service person in the civil courts if a breach of contract or an 'actionable' misrepresentation has taken place (see pp. 15 and 65). The rules are the same as for the spoken word.

■ A solicitor booked a skiing holiday on the basis of what was said in a brochure published by a firm of travel agents. Various attractions were promised, including '. . . Welcome party on arrival. Afternoon tea and cake for 7 days. Swiss dinner by candlelight. Fondue party. Yodler evening . . .' The brochure also stated: 'You will be in for a great time when you book this houseparty holiday. Mr Weibel, the charming owner, speaks English.'

Sounds like fun but it wasn't. There was no welcome party. The cake for tea was only potato crisps and dry nutcake. The yodler evening consisted of a local man in his working clothes singing a few songs very quickly. By the second week the solicitor was the only member of the 'houseparty' left and, as the 'charming owner' did not after all speak English, there was no one to whom the lone guest could talk. The solicitor sued the travel agents on his return to the UK. The court held that he was entitled to be compensated for the loss of entertainment and enjoyment which he had been promised but had not received. (Jarvis v Swan Tours Ltd (1973) 1 AE 72)

The service person could possibly be prosecuted by the local authority for breach of the Trade Descriptions Act. Again, the rules are the same as for the spoken word (see p. 66).

■ A man paid in advance for an 'early bird' airline ticket. The airline wrote to him confirming his reservation on a particular flight on a particular date. The man did not know that the airline operated a policy of deliberately overbooking to avoid flying with empty seats. When the man turned up for the flight there was no room for him on it. The airline was prosecuted and the court decided that the letter sent to the man did amount to a false statement within the meaning of the Section 14 of the Trade Descriptions Act. The airline would therefore have been found guilty were it not for the fact that the letter was sent by BOAC, which had become British Airways by the time of the prosecution. On this basis only they were acquitted. (British Airways Board v Taylor 1976 1 WLR 13)

A consumer who is annoyed or offended by a particular advertisement can complain about it if the advertisement contravenes the ASA or IBA codes, both of which cover advertisements about services as well as goods (see p. 22).

Written agreements

As already explained in relation to the sale of goods (see p. 25), a written agreement does not have to be in any particular form to be effective and the same applies to the sale of services. (For instance, in the case quoted above the promises contained in the brochure amounted to contract terms.) It is true again that the written word will usually take precedence over anything allegedly said at the time the agreement was made. Therefore it is always better to make a written record of what was agreed and get the service person to sign it as well as signing it yourself. As will be seen later, the Supply of Goods and Services Act (which does not apply in Scotland) does make some provision about price and time if neither are agreed, but these provisions are rather vague and a precise written agreement will protect you much better.

When drafting your agreement use the legal phrase 'time is of the essence' (see p. 41) so that there can be no doubt that the service person is legally bound to finish the job within a particular time. When dealing with the price it is better to be absolutely definite, or you may find yourself landed with a bill that is much higher than expected. The expressions 'quotation' or 'estimate' may be used. Although neither have a recognized legal meaning, it is considered that an estimate is merely an inspired guess as to how much a job will cost and therefore not much use to you legally. A quotation, however, should represent a more definite statement of the price to be charged. It is probably better to avoid the use of either expression and simply state in plain English that particular work is to be done for a particular price within a particular time. For example, 'It is agreed that a wooden wardrobe made of pine, dimensions ___ is to be built and installed in my bedroom at a price of ___ to be completed by ___. Time is of the essence.'

It may well be that the service person has drawn up an agreement for you to sign. However boring the prospect of ploughing through yards of small print may be, it is vital that you make absolutely sure that there is nothing in the agreement which could be prejudicial to your interests. As will be explained later, the law does operate to exclude particularly unfair terms when you are dealing with a businessperson but you should still read what you are signing and cross out items you do not want included.

Service persons who do not adhere to an agreement made with a consumer can be sued for breach of contract, and the consumer can claim either the right to set the contract aside completely (called recission by lawyers) and/or damages depending on whether the term was a condition or warranty (or material in Scotland) (see *Legal explanation*). The same applies to both oral and written contracts but if the agreement is not in writing its existence is obviously much more difficult to prove.

Fine print

In the section on buying goods we we explained how the Unfair Contract Terms Act 1977 operates to invalidate certain provisions (called 'exclusion' or 'exemption' clauses by lawyers) by which traders might attempt to evade their responsibilities to consumers. This Act also applies to exclusion clauses that might be used in relation to services. (The Act does not apply to certain types of service, e.g. insurance contracts.)

As with goods, the Act provides that some exclusion clauses are to have no effect at all and others only if a court would consider them 'reasonable'. The following clauses in relation to services are legally of no effect at all.*

- Exclusion clauses cannot be used to limit a trader's responsibilities to a consumer in respect of the quality of goods provided with a service, their fitness for the required purpose nor in respect of any misdescription of the goods.
- Service persons cannot use an exclusion clause to avoid responsibility for death or injury caused by their negligence (delict in Scotland).

The following exclusion clauses will be of legal effect only if a court would consider them reasonable. (See p. 28 for what 'reasonable' means in this context and note the example below.)

- Clauses in any contract with a consumer for services will be excluded in the same circumstances as with contracts for the purchase of goods. (See p. 27 for the provisions in question.)
- Exclusion clauses that deal with misrepresentation will be excluded in the same circumstances as when goods are bought. (See p. 27 for the provisions in question.)
- Exclusion clauses by which service persons try to avoid responsibility for economic loss or damage caused by their negligence will be of no effect unless reasonable.

■ A man agreed with British Rail that they would transport his suitcase from Stockport to Haverfordwest by rail at 'owner's risk' for £6.03. There was a standard form contract which contained a widely drafted exemption clause exempting British Rail from responsibility for any loss, misdelivery, damage or delay unless the customer could prove wilful misconduct by British Rail. An exemption clause also provided that, if the goods failed to arrive at all, any financial compensation was to be limited to a sum which related to the weight of the goods. This would have meant that, if the case failed to arrive, the man would have got only £27 as opposed to the actual value of the case and contents which was £320.32. The case did fail to arrive and the man sued British Rail. The court decided that the exclusion clause was not 'reasonable' and the man was awarded

---

* In Scotland the Act only applies to exclusion clauses contained in a contract; in the rest of the UK it also applies to exclusion clauses contained in notices which are not part of the actual contract.

the £320.32. (Waldron Kelly v British Railways Board (1981) 3CL 33 (Stockport County Court))

Shoddy service

A consumer may be dissatisfied with a service because the work in question has not been done properly. For example, a roof that has supposedly been repaired may leak as soon as it rains or a watch that has supposedly been cleaned may cease to function the day after collection.

Even if there was no written or verbal agreement a consumer still has some rights in such situations. For some time it has been established by various court decisions that a service person has a duty to use such degree of care and skill as could be reasonably expected when carrying out a service. Now these rights are contained in a statute (see below) except in Scotland where the law is still based on decided court cases.

Shoddy service goods

If goods are supplied as part of a service (e.g. a plumber may both install and supply piping) then the Supply of Goods and Services Act 1982 provides that the service person is under the same duty to provide goods that are of 'merchantable quality' and fit for the required purpose as is the seller of goods alone. This is stated in Section 4 of the Act but this protection applies only if the service person is a businessperson. The rules are exactly the same as when goods only are being sold (see p. 29).

The Sale of Goods and Services Act does not apply in Scotland but in decided court cases it has been established that materials used must be of 'sound quality and reasonably fit for the purpose'.*

As already mentioned, a service person cannot evade responsibility for breach of these duties by means of an exclusion clause.

Shoddy service

Section 13 of the Suppy of Goods and Services Act 1982 (which

---

* David M. Walker, *Principles of Scottish Private Law*, 3rd edition, Vol. I, p. 289. Also it might be possible for Scottish consumers to rely on the Sale of Goods Act.

does not apply in Scotland) states: 'In a contract for the supply of a service, where the supplier is acting in the course of a business there is an implied term that the supplier will carry out the service with *reasonable care and skill*.' This means that if a service is not carried out with reasonable care and skill a dissatisfied consumer can sue a business service person for breach of this section. Most of the cases on this subject were heard before the Act was passed but it is assumed that the principles stated in them would still apply.

■ A customer took a motor car to a firm of motor repairers to have the braking system repaired. It was agreed on the recommendation of the repairers that certain parts of the brakes should be sent to a particular 'specialist' for relining. After this expert treatment the car was later damaged in an accident due, it was found, to the unsuitable linings fitted and faulty work carried out by the so-called specialists. The customer won the case. The court held that the customer had relied on the repairers to repair the brakes of the car in a suitable and efficient manner and that it was the duty of the repairers to provide good workmanship and materials of good quality and a braking system that was reasonably fit for the purpose. (Note that the repairers were liable even though the 'specialists' did the work and were responsible not just for the shoddy service but also for the shoddy brake linings.) (Stewart v Reavells Garage 2 QB 545 1952)

Section 12 of this Act provides that the government may pass regulations exempting certain classes of service persons from their obligations under this section. It may come as no surprise to know that so far one category of person exempted are advocates (these will usually be lawyers) when performing in a court, tribunal, inquiry or arbitration and when carrying out preliminary work directly affecting the conduct of the hearing. Also excused are arbitrators and umpires.

In Scotland where the Act does not apply it has been established in various court cases that services must be done in a 'tradesman-like manner' and professionals must 'use a fair and reasonable standard of professional knowledge, skill and care, such as is possessed and used by the normally skilled and competent member of the profession or trade in question'.*

---

* David M. Walker, *Principles of Scottish Private Law*, 3rd edition, Vol. II, pp. 284 and 289.

As already mentioned (see p. 69) any attempt by service persons to use an exclusion clause to evade their responsibilities to a consumer for breach of contract or negligence resulting in economic loss would be of no effect unless considered 'reasonable' by a court. Performing a shoddy service could amount to either breach of contract or negligence. In some cases where bad professional advice was given, persons who did not themselves make a contract with the adviser but nevertheless suffered loss as a result of the advice given, have recovered damages for negligence. (See case on p. 81.) This is a difficult area of law and advice should be taken.

Dangerous service

If a service is not performed properly then not only economic loss but also injury may result. Those injured may not be the ones who actually commissioned the service. For example, a lift that has not been serviced properly and is left in a dangerous state may cause injury to a user who has had nothing to do with the service contract. If a service is performed in a dangerous way then anyone injured as a result may have the right to sue the service person. As already mentioned under *Fine print*, service persons cannot use an exclusion clause to evade liability for death or injury caused by a bad service and in the case of economic loss such a clause would only be effective if considered 'reasonable'.

Breach of contract

The person who made the actual agreement to have the service performed could sue for breach of contract if s/he was injured or suffered economic loss as a result of a dangerous service. In England, Wales and Northern Ireland the consumer could sue for breach of Section 13 of the Supply of Goods and Services Act (see p. 22). The statute implies into the contract between consumer and business service person a term that the service be performed with reasonable care and skill. Obviously a service which was done so badly that injury resulted would very probably be in breach of this section. In Scotland a consumer could sue for breach of contract on the basis that the service was not performed to the standard demanded by common law (see p. 72).

Persons who did not make the actual agreement with the service person probably could not sue for breach of contract but might be able to sue for negligence.

■ A man and his brother went to have a Turkish bath and spent the night on beds in cubicles provided there. In the morning they woke to find they had been badly bitten by bugs. They sued the owners of the baths both for breach of contract and for negligence. The owners argued that they were not in breach of contract because there was no implied term in the contract to the effect that customers should not be bitten. They also argued they had not been negligent as they had taken all reasonable care to ensure the premises were bug-free. The customers won the case. The court held that the owners were in breach of contract as the beds should have been reasonably fit for the purpose and the owners owed a duty to customers to take reasonable care that no bugs or dangerous insects should infest their premises. The court also held the owners were negligent as the knew of the danger of infestation and had not taken precautions that were sufficient. (This case show how a consumer can sue both for breach of contract and negligence. Although decided before the Supply of Goods and Services Act, it is thought that the same principles still apply.) (Silverman v Imperial London Hotels Ltd 1927 137 LT 57)

Negligence

Negligence (or delict in Scotland) is the legal term for careless-ness. On p. 35 we explained in what situations consumers are able to sue sellers and manufacturers of goods for their careless actions. The same rules apply to service persons, who can be sued for negligence if the same circumstances apply. This means that anyone injured as a result of the careless actions of a service person will be able to sue if they can prove that the injury to them was 'reasonably foreseeable.'

A solicitor's clerk was going to visit a client who was a tenant of a fifth-floor flat. The clerk was shown into the lift in the block of flats in question by a porter employed by the landlord. When the lift reached second floor it stopped and began to descend. The descent increased in speed until the lift stopped with a violent jerk at the bottom of the basement. As a result of this unpleasant occurrence the clerk suffered a spinal injury. It later transpired that the lift had behaved in this fashion because the cylinder gland had broken and this in turn had occurred as a result of faulty repair work performed by a mechanic employed by a firm of engineers who were under contract to the landlord to keep the lift in order. The court held that the firm of engineers were liable to pay damages to the clerk as, through their negligence, the lift had been left in a dangerous condition. (Note that they were liable even though the clerk had no contract with them. Injuries to him were reasonably forseeable.) (Haseldine v Daw and Sons Ltd (1941) 2 KB 343 and 3AE 156 CA)

Criminal Prosecution

Although the sale of goods in a dangerous condition can sometimes lead to a prosecution in the criminal courts, there is no general legislation to protect the consumer against the sale of dangerous services. However, it is a criminal offence to alter a motor vehicle or trailer so as to make either unroadworthy; or to fit a part to a vehicle which would result in its use on the road being unlawful (Road Traffic Acts).

It is also a criminal offence to sell unfit food (see p. 18 for legislation). Thus restaurants serving up dangerous meals can be prosecuted (see example on p. 38). Also, the government can make regulations to secure the observance of sanitary and clean conditions and practices in respect of the sale, preparation and service of food. This includes the prohibition of spitting on premises where food is sold for human consumption! Unhygienic caterers can be banned from using the premises in question for catering. In England, Scotland and Wales it is a criminal offence to install an unsafe gas appliance (see p. 111 for more details).

Other problems

No service or late service

As explained on p. 68, it is far better when paying out for a service to make a written agreement as to how long the service is to take. If you do this and service persons do not keep to their side of the bargain then they can be sued for breach of contract. If no written or verbal agreement is made then the consumer has the following rights:

- The supply of Goods and Services Act 1982 (which does not apply in Scotland) provides in Section 14 that there is to be 'an implied term that the supplier will carry out the service within a reasonable time'. The section also states: 'What is a reasonable time is a question of fact.' This means that if a service is not performed within a reasonable time then a consumer can sue for breach of this term. (See example below for an idea of what a court might consider to be unreasonable.)

● In Scotland it has been decided in court cases that if no time is specified for completion then the work must be done 'within a time reasonable in the circumstances'.*

● Business service persons throughout the UK cannot evade their responsibilities for late service by means of an exclusion clause unless such an attempt would be considered reasonable (see p. 70).

■ A man took his car to a garage for repairs on the basis that his insurance company (which had already approved the garage's estimate) would foot the bill. The man had overheard the garage manager tell the insurance assessor that the garage was very busy but no one told the man that there would be any delay in respect of his car. Whilst the repairs were being done the man hired a car. The garage took eight weeks to finish the repairs because they were short of skilled staff, the situation being aggravated by staff taking holidays. The man was able to prove that in normal circumstances a competent repairer could have done the job in five weeks. The court held the garage must compensate the man for three weeks' hire of the car. They were under a contractual duty to him to do the job within a reasonable time. (Charnock v Liverpool Corporation (1968) 1 WLR 1498)

No price or the wrong price

As explained on p. 68, it is far better when paying out for a service to make a clear written agreement about the price and what work is to be done for that price. That way you avoid the difficulty of situations where a service person wants to be paid more for the work than you think is reasonable or claims that you asked for a

---

* David M. Walker, *Principles of Scottish Private Law*, 3rd edition, Vol. II, p. 290.

much bigger job than you actually intended. If no written or verbal agreement is made about price then the consumer has the following rights:

- The Supply of Goods and Services Act 1982 (which does not apply in Scotland) provides in Section 15 that, in the absence of an agreement, there is to be an 'implied term that the party contracting with the supplier will pay a reasonable charge'. Later on the section states: 'What is a reasonable charge is a question of fact.' This means that a service person can only legally demand a 'reasonable' price for the service they have performed. What is and what is not reasonable is debatable but if you could prove that somebody else with the same skills would be prepared to charge less you should be in a strong position.
- In Scotland it has been established in decided court cases that if no price is fixed 'the obligation is to pay a reasonable price for the work'.*
- If you make clear to service persons exactly what work you want done then that does not give them carte blanche to do other jobs for you that you have not requested. Unfortunately, if there is nothing in writing it will be your word against theirs as to what you actually did ask them to do. Legally though you are only obliged to pay for the work you asked to be done.

Your goods in their hands

If you leave your property with a service person for work to be done on it then the service person is under a legal duty to take reasonable care of your goods. This principle has been established in various court cases. Sometimes service persons try to evade this responsibility by means of an exclusion clause but such attempts would only succeed if a court would consider the clause 'reasonable'. In the example quoted on p. 70 the judge also said that in a case where non-delivery of goods had occurred the onus was on the bailees (the legal term for someone who is looking after someone else's property) to show that the loss was not their fault and that British Rail had failed to do this.

---

* David M. Walker, *Principles of Scottish Private Law*, 3rd edition, Vol. II, p. 292.

■ A man left his boat in dry dock for repairs. There was a remarkably high tide, the dock gates burst open and as a result the boat was damaged. There was only one watchman looking out after the boats although it was day-time. The court held that the dry dock owner must compensate the boat owner for the damage. It was the dock owner's duty to have sufficient men in the dock to take precautions when danger was approaching. (Leck v Maestaer (1807) 1 Camp 138)

If a customer leaves goods with a service person for work to be done to them and then refuses to pay, the service person is legally entitled to retain the goods until payment is made. The service person's right is called a 'lien' by lawyers and covers money owed for materials supplied and work performed (but not warehousing or storage charge). The right to a lien has been established in various court cases.

If you leave goods with a service person for work to be done and then fail to return to collect them then the Torts (Interference with Goods) Act 1977 (which does not apply in Scotland) states that in certain circumstances the service person may sell the goods and account to you for the difference. To be able to take advantage of this Act the service person must either give you something in writing when you leave the goods obliging you to return to collect them or later send or deliver to you a written notice to say that the goods are ready to be collected, specifying where they should be collected from and how much is owed. The service person must also send to you by registered post or recorded delivery a 'notice of intention to sell' the goods. This must specify where the goods are, how much you owe and how much time you have before s/he will sell them. (If you owe money for work done s/he must give you at least three months.)

In Scotland the statute to cover this situation no longer exists. Scottish common law states that abandoned property belongs to the Crown and there is a statutory procedure for disposing of it.

Stolen service goods

If goods supplied with a service turn out to be stolen then the consumer can sue the service person for breach of Section 2 of the Supply of Goods and Services Act. The Act (which does not apply in Scotland) provides that the person supplying goods with a service is presumed to have the right to sell them. The same protection applies as when goods only are sold (see p. 59).

In Scotland aggrieved consumers would have to rely on Scottish common law provisions or on the Sale of Goods Act.

5.

The professionals

If a consumer consult a professional person such as a doctor or lawyer then the consumer has basically the same rights as when employing other sorts of service persons. However, many people on being aggrieved by a bad service provided by a professional come up against a giant psychological barrier. There is a feeling that nothing can be done, that other professionals will band together to support the offender, that there will be a successful 'cover-up'. This is not so. It *is* possible to obtain redress against the professionals. It can and has been done.

It is not possible to deal with all professional groups so we have selected those you are most likely to have dealings with, namely lawyers, medical personnel and professionals concerned with residential property, such as estate agents and surveyors. (Financial services are dealt with on pp. 99–105.) The activities of some professionals are controlled by specific statutes and most have disciplinary bodies prepared to consider complaints against their members. Professionals have, however, shown a lack of enthusiasm in establishing independent complaints procedures.

Lawyers

Most people need legal advice at some time. If you are accused of a crime, want to get divorced, sue for damages after a road accident, make a will, buy a house or seek consumer advice, these are all matters for which you may want expert help. You may decide to consult a qualified lawyer or you may seek help elsewhere, e.g. from a Citizens Advice Bureau.

The qualified side of the legal profession in the UK is comprised of solicitors and barristers (called advocates in Scotland). Together they have the monopoly of the right to conduct court cases for money. Barristers have the sole right to speak for money in the higher courts but the consumer can only approach them via a solicitor. (Solicitors have been given minor rights of audience in certain very restricted circumstances.) This of course means paying for both, and can prove expensive. Indeed, during the course of one case (that of Porter v General Guarantee Corporation Ltd, 1982), the judge remarked: 'Whatever be the effect of my judgement, it may well be that everyone will be out of pocket except the lawyers who have all conducted their respective cases with skill and dedication and have thoroughly earned their fees. No one could say that their work was not of merchantable quality.' (Whether or not those paying for the fees agreed with the last sentiment is not recorded.)

Solicitors also at present have a monopoly over the right to charge money to do conveyancing; this is shortly to be abolished although there will be legal controls over who else can do it. Legal aid is available to consumers on a means-tested basis (see p. 168) for the services of barristers and solicitors but not for the services of other types of legal advisers.

Solicitors

The behaviour of solicitors is subject to some statutory control (the Solicitors Act 1974, England and Wales) and the day-to-day responsibility for enforcing the provisions of this Act and for supervising solicitors generally has been given to the Law Society. (The Law Society also acts as a quasi trade union for many solicitors, and it has been suggested that for the same body to fulfil both functions is not really appropriate.)

Suing your solicitor

Solicitors, like any other service person, can be sued for breach of contract or negligence if they do not conduct their clients' affairs to the standard required. Solicitors have a duty to be skilful and careful *but*, like other advocates, they cannot be sued for bad advocacy or bad court preparation (see p. 83 for more details). Solicitors are not allowed to act for people unless they are insured against negligence claims so a solicitor is always worth suing. The Law Society does not investigate allegations of negligence but it does run a 'negligence panel' where solicitors will give you up to an hour's worth of free advice about whether it is worth suing your solicitor for negligence. If you require this service, write to The Secretary, Professional Purposes, The Law Society, 8 Breams Buildings, London EC4A 1HP.

■ A man asked a solicitor to draw up a will in which he wanted something to be left to his sister-in-law. The solicitor sent the will to the man to be signed and witnessed, but omitted to mention that if anyone married to a proposed beneficiary was used as a witness that beneficiary would get nothing. The gift to them would then in law be invalid. The sister-in-law's husband witnessed the will, but the solicitor failed to notice this when the will was returned to him. Two years later the man died and nine months after that the solicitor informed the sister-in-law that she would get nothing because her husband had witnessed the will. She sued for damages.

   The solicitor argued that he was responsible only to his client (who was of course dead) but not to her. The sister-in-law won the case and the court held that the solicitor was under a duty to her to use proper care in carrying out the dead man's instructions. The solicitor had been negligent. (Ross v Caunters 1979 3 AE 580)

Your money in their hands

If you are not eligible for legal aid solicitors will probably ask for money in advance before starting a case for you. If they do so then your money should be kept by them in a separate 'client account'. The Solicitors Act also states that where interest ought in fairness to be earned on your money then the solicitor must either put it somewhere where it will attract interest or pay you an equivalent sum. At present the Solicitors Accounts (Deposit Interest) Rules 1975 state that if the sum handed over to the solicitor exceeds £500 and is unlikely to be diminished below that figure within two months then the client should receive some interest. If a solicitor runs off with your money then you can ask the Law Society for compensation: all practising solicitors pay annually into a compensation funds set up specifically for this purpose.

Your bill

If you think your solicitor's bill is too high you can ask a court officer to 'tax', i.e. check it for you. The disadvantage of this is that there is a fee payable for the service. If the matter has not gone through the courts (called 'non-contentious') you can ask the Law Society to check the bill free of charge. (If you agreed to the fee in question before the solicitor did the work then the Law Society may not be prepared to look into it.) The Solicitors' Renumeration Order 1972 states that the charge should be 'fair and reasonable having regard to all the circumstances of the case'. Solicitors should not sue for their money unless you have first been told of your rights to go to the Law Society if no taxation has taken place.

Complaining about solicitors

In England and Wales if you cannot sue a solicitor but want to complain about his/her behaviour you can consider reporting the solicitor to the Law Society at the address given above. The Law Society is prepared to investigate allegations against solicitors of persistent delay in answering letters, failure to account for money held on a client's behalf, failure to keep a client's affairs confidential, improperly acting for two people whose interests conflict, taking advantage of a client's age or inexperience, overcharging and dishonesty. If the Law Society considers your complaint is well founded, solicitors can be taken to a disciplinary tribunal can which fine them (but the money does not go to the consumer!) or prevent them from practising as solicitors. If the Law Society decides your complaint is not well founded it will take no further action but if you still feel aggrieved you can complain about that to the Lay Observer, Royal Courts of Justice, Strand, London WC2. There is a *three-month time limit*, which runs from the end of the Law Society's investigation, after which you lose your right to complain to the Lay Observer. If s/he thinks your complaint is justified s/he will make recommendations to the Law Society who ought to take note of them.

Scotland and Northern Ireland have separate Law Societies of their own and separate legislation (the Solicitors (Northern Ireland) Order 1976 and the Solicitors (Scotland) Act 1980 as amended). It follows that some of what has been said above does not apply to these countries. The position is broadly similar though but for more information contact the relevant Law Society. In Scotland complaints against solicitors can be made to the Law Society of Scotland, 26–27 Drunsheagh Gardens, Edinburgh EH3 7YR. In Northern Ireland the address is the Law Society of Northern Ireland, 90 Victoria Street, Belfast BT1 3GN.

Barristers

Barristers are not subject to any statutory control but they do have a code of conduct to which each barrister should adhere. Barristers' behaviour (in England and Wales) is supervised by the Senate of the Inns of Court and the Bar, 11 South Square, Gray's Inn, London WC1.

Suing a barrister

It is not easy to sue barristers for bad service because they enjoy a unique immunity from actions for negligence. Neither can they be sued by a consumer for breach of contract because they are not considered in law to have any contract with those they represent, or even with the solicitor. (In any event, 'advocates' are exempted from the relevant provisions in the supply of Goods and Services Act, see p. 72). It has been decided in various court cases that a barrister cannot be sued for negligent advocacy in court nor for negligent preparation of paperwork connected with court proceedings. Judges (the vast majority of whom are barristers themselves) have justified this exceptional treatment of their fellows on grounds of 'public policy'.

■ A man was charged with the offence of intentionally causing grievous bodily harm to another. He sued the barrister who defended him a court for negligent conduct of his defence. The court held that the barrister was immune from being sued on this basis. (Rondel v Worsley (1967) 993 3 AE)

However, if barristers give negligent advice before a court case has actually begun they could possibly be sued successfully for negligence. Like solicitors, barristers have to be insured against such claims and therefore are always worth suing. If the barrister cannot be sued it is possible that you might be able to sue the solicitor instead, but this is a difficult area of law and it would be best to get advice.

Barristers' fees

Barristers are not considered in law to have a contract with either the solicitor or the client so they are not allowed to sue for their fees. However, in practice, solicitors who do not pay a barrister they have instructed are pressurized to pay up and will probably therefore pressurize the client for what they have paid the barrister. As you will see below, the Bar Senate can, following disciplinary proceedings against a barrister, order the latter to forgo or repay fees.

Complaining about barristers

In **England and Wales** complaints about professional misconduct or 'conduct unbecoming a barrister' can be sent to the Bar Council at the address given. The code of conduct obliges a barrister to 'uphold the interests of his client without regard to his own interests or to any consequences to himself or to any other person'. A barrister also has a duty of confidentiality to his/her client. On receiving any complaint, the Committee of the Senate will either decide to take no action, refer the complaint to the Treasurer of the barrister's Inn or bring the barrister before the Senate Disciplinary Committee. The committee can disbar or suspend barristers from practising, order them to forgo and repay fees or reprimand them.

Scotland and Northern Ireland have their own separate professional bodies: the Faculty of Advocates in Scotland, Parliament House, Edinburgh EH1 1RF, and the Complaints Committee of the Bar Executive Council in Northern Ireland, Bar Library, Royal Courts of Justice, Belfast BT1 3JF.

Other legal advisers

Anyone who is not a solicitor or barrister but who nevertheless offers legal advice and then does so carelessly can be sued for either breach of contract or negligence.

When the provisions about conveyancing have come into effect, non-solicitor conveyancers will have to be licensed. A Council for Licensed Conveyancers has been established which will investigate complaints about licensed conveyancers and take away the licenses of those who behave badly. Licensed conveyancers will also have to be insured. It is possible that certain recognized institutions such as building societies will be permitted to do conveyancing.

Health professionals

Everyone needs expert advice about some aspect of their health at one time or another. A consumer may go to a doctor, dentist or optician either privately or under the NHS. Some people prefer to consult other sorts of health professionals such as osteopaths, homoeopaths or herbalists.

Suing for negligence or breach of contract

Any person who claims to the public to be ready to give medical advice is assumed to have enough skill and knowledge for that purpose. Therefore, a consumer who has consulted such a person and failed to receive a sufficiently skilful service can sue the person for breach of contract or negligence. Problems arise, particularly in the medical field, when a consumer is injured and there is a disagreement within the health profession about whether what was done was correct or not. As the law stands at present, to pursue an action for medical negligence successfully, a consumer would have to prove that the person adopted a course of treatment that no professional person of ordinary skill would reasonably have adopted at that time. In other words, if a doctor, for example, can show that other reputable doctors agree that what s/he did was reasonable then the consumer will not be awarded damages (even if other reputable doctors disagree).

■ A man who suffered from mental illness was advised and agreed to undergo ECT. No relaxant drugs or manual restraint were used when the treatment was administered, although male nurses stood on either side of the couch. The man suffered severe physical injuries consisting of dislocation of both hip joints with fractures of the pelvis on each side caused by the head of the femur being driven through the cup on the pelvis. At that time opinion differed within the medical profession as to whether relaxant drugs or manual restraint should be used when a patient was having ECT. The court held therefore that the man's doctor had not been negligent in using neither. (Bolam v Friern Hospital Management Committee (1957) 2 AE 118)

However, large numbers of people have claimed successfully for medical negligence so it is by no means impossible. Recently, for example, there was a claim by a woman who had had a sterilization operation. After the operation she became pregnant, refused to have an abortion and later gave birth to a child with congenital deformities. She sued the health authority and was awarded damages. (Emeh v Kensington and Chelsea and Westminster Area Health Authority, 1984 3AE 1044)

Criminal prosecution

With the object of protecting the public from the attentions of bogus health professionals, legislation has been passed limiting the extent to which unqualified persons can offer and give medical attention to people. A person who claims to be qualified to give medical treatment when in fact s/he has not got the qualifications in question or the qualifications which the law demands before treatment of that sort can legally be given, can be liable to criminal prosecution.

For example, under the Medical Act 1983 it is a criminal offence for a person falsely to represent that s/he is registered as a qualified medical practitioner although it is not unlawful for unqualified persons to practise medicine if they do not make such a pretence. However, the statute does provide that non-registered persons cannot sue for medical fees. It is also an offence under the Nurses, Midwives and Health Visitors Act 1979 falsely to claim with intent to deceive to be a qualified nurse, midwife or health visitor. Under the Dentists Act 1984, however, it *is* an offence to practise dentistry without being qualified. The Opticians Act 1958 provides that only qualified opthalmic opticians may test eyes. Unqualified persons may now sell spectacles but not other opthalmic appliances such as contact lenses. Only registered dispensers of hearing aids may dispense them (Hearing Aid Council Act 1968). The Veterinary Surgeons Act 1966 states that it is an offence for an unqualified person to practise veterinary surgery.

Complaints and removal of undesirables

Many health professionals have to be registered with some central body in order to be permitted to practise. The central bodies have powers to strike practitioners off their registers following convictions for certain criminal offences, for serious professional misconduct (the categories of which are not strictly defined) or for becoming physically or mentally unfit to practise. They also publish guidelines to indicate what level of conduct is expected. (Complaints relating to the NHS and alternative medicine are covered later.)

Doctors can be removed from circulation by the General Medical Council, 44 Hallam Street, London W1. Examples of behaviour the GMC say they would not approve include failure to visit a patient when necessary and improper disclosure of information about a patient.

Dentists are supervised by the General Dental Council, 37 Wimpole Street, London W1M 8DQ. Tel: 01–486 2171. The Council would not approve, amongst other things: treatment of patients under general anaesthetic or sedation without adhering to the correct procedures; making misleading statements, such as inducing a patient to pay for private treatment by falsely suggesting that the same could not be carried out under the NHS, and improper delegation to non-qualified persons.

Nurses, midwives and health visitors are supervised by the United

Kingdom Central Council for Nursing, Midwifery and Health Visiting, 23 Portland Place, London W1N 3AF. Tel: 01–637 7181. They expect amongst other things that these professionals maintain a respect for confidential information and also that they take into account the customs, values and spiritual beliefs of patients.

Opticians can be prevented from practising by the General Optical Council, 41 Harley Street, London W1. The British College of Ophthalmic Opticians publishes a code of ethics which, amongst other things, obliges members to charge reasonably and not to undertake work such as fitting contact lenses without adequate training and experience. The Complaints Bureau of the Association of Optical Practitioners (about three-quarters of practising ophthalmic opticians are members) (233 Blackfriars Road, London SE1 8NW. Tel: 01–261 9661) will investigate complaints about treatment, optical appliances and charges. If you write in, a copy of your letter will be sent to the optician concerned requesting his/her comments. The bureau might recommend that the optician make you a refund.

Vets can be struck off by the Royal College of Veterinary Surgeons, 32 Belgrave Square, London SW1. Tel: 01–235 4971.

The National Health Service (NHS)

The problem of finding that you need treatment but that either that particular treatment is not available or that there is a long waiting list for it under the NHS, is becoming all too common. Can the NHS be forced to treat you? The National Health Service Act 1977 imposes various duties on the Secretary of State for Social Services. (In Scotland the National Health Service (Scotland) Act 1978 makes similar provisions and in Ireland similar duties are imposed on the Ministry of Health and Social Services.) Section 1(1) of the Act states that s/he has a duty to

> continue the promotion in England and Wales of a comprehensive health service designed to secure improvement (a) in the physical and mental health of the people of those countries; and (b) in the preventation, diagnosis and treatment of illness: and for that purpose to provide or secure the effective provision of services . . .

The Act also states that the Secretary of State must, amongst other things, provide:

to such extent as he considers necessary to meet all reasonable requirements, hospital accommodation, medical, dental, nursing and ambulance services, facilities for the care of expectant and nursing mothers and young children and facilities for the prevention of illness and after-care and such other facilities as are required for the diagnosis and treatment of illness.

There has been speculation as to whether aggrieved patients could sue the Secretary of State for breach of these statutory duties if treatment is denied or delayed under the NHS. At the moment it can only be said that there are considerable obstacles and that in one case so far the patients failed (see example below). This does not mean though that someone else should not try.

■ Four orthopaedic patients who had been kept waiting for treatment started a court case against the Secretary of State for Social Services on the basis that he was in breach of his duties under the National Health Service Act. The Court of Appeal ruled that the patients had no cause of action under the Act. (R v Secretary of State for Social Services ex parte Hincks CA (1980) – unreported)

If you want to complain about something the NHS has or has not done then there are established mechanisms by which you can do so. A complaint about bad service by a GP, dentist, chemist, or optician can be made to your local Family Practitioner Committee (FPC) (Secretary of the Health Board in Scotland; Chief Administrative Officer of the Local Health and Social Services Board in Northern Ireland) but this must be done no later than eight weeks (six in Scotland and Northern Ireland) after the event you want to complain about. (With dentists you have eight weeks after you realized something was wrong or six months after the end of the course of treatment, whichever is the soonest.) The FPC will try and resolve the matter informally and will hold a hearing only if the matter might amount to a breach of the practitioner's 'terms of service'. If there is a hearing you will be invited to it. If your complaint is substantiated the practitioner may be warned or lose pay, but the money is not given to the patient! You might, however, be reimbursed for extra expenditure on treatment you have incurred because of the bad treatment in question. In addition or instead, of course, practitioners can be reported to their disciplinary body.

Complaints about hospital organization or bad medical

treatment in hospital should be made first to the person responsible. If that does not resolve matters the patient has the right to have the issue considered by a more senior member of staff. If that fails, then ultimately either the health authority (in the case of bad organization) or the regional medical officer (in the case of bad treatment) will have to enquire into the matter, and other consultants may be called in to give their opinions. There is also a Health Service ombudsman (the Health Service Commissioner) who will investigate complaints that an individual has suffered injustice or hardship as a result of alleged bad service or failure to provide a service which a health authority is under a duty to provide. The ombudsman will not deal with allegations of bad exercise of clinical judgement and will expect you to have first exhausted your rights under the complaints procedure or to go to court if appropriate. The ombudsman will not look into complaints against doctors, dentists, pharmacists or opticians as the FPC deals with these, but can look into the way the FPC dealt with a complaint under their 'informal' procedure. You must complain to the ombudsman within a year of the event complained about. If the ombudsman agrees that your complaint comes within his/her jurisdiction then you will ultimately be sent a written report giving the findings and telling you, if s/he agreed you had a point, what remedy the health authority has agreed on.

If you need help to present your complaint then you can consult your local Community Health Council (look in the phone book for their address) and they will advise you. (In Scotland consult the Local Health Council, in Northern Ireland your Area Board). Community Health Councils were established to represent the interests of consumers of the National Health Service. They will advise consumers about all their various rights and treatments available under the NHS, not all of which can be listed here.

Alternative medicine

Some people prefer to turn to what is sometimes called 'alternative' medicine at times of illness. Such treatments are not specifically legally controlled in that there is no statutorily established body with the responsibility of registering and disciplining practitioners of such treatments. As long as the criminal law is not broken (see p. 86) anyone can set themselves up as an alternative medical practitioner but such people can be sued for negligence and breach of contract just like registered doctors. However, in the absence of a reliable recommendation you might well be advised to make sure the person you consult is properly qualified. You might be able to obtain some alternative treatments under NHS, but it could be difficult to find an NHS practitioner with the necessary skills and inclination to offer you such treatments.

Acupuncture

The Council of Acupuncture, 10 Belgrave Square, London SW1X 8PH, publishes a Register of British Acupuncturists which lists those who have been through recognized training courses. The Council also sets standards of ethical conduct. Sometimes it is possible to get acupuncture on the NHS. The British Medical Acupuncture Society, 67/69 Chancery Lane, London WC2 1AF, will send a list (but only to your GP) of doctors qualified to perform acupuncture treatments.

Herbalists

Some herbalists are trained and are members of the National Institute of Medical Herbalists, 41 Hatherly Road, Winchester, Hants SO22 6RR. Tel: 0962 68776. The practice of herbalism is now coming under government scrutiny as the dispensing of some herbal medicines is being controlled under the Medicines Act 1968. The Act permits only licensed persons, e.g. qualified pharmacists, to dispense controlled medical products.

Homoeopathy

Homoeopathy has always been available under the NHS but not many doctors practise it. For information about doctors who do, write to the Faculty of Homoeopathy, The Royal Homoeopathic Hospital, Great Ormond Street, London WC1N 3VR. Tel: 01–837 8833. There are a number of qualified homoeopaths who are not also doctors. The Society of Homoeopaths, Shenfield, Brentwood, Essex CM15 8PP, has information about these.

Osteopathy and Chiropractic

The establishment seems to have accepted the use of such treatments but there are very few doctors qualified as osteopaths and therefore it is virtually impossible to obtain osteopathy under the NHS. Details of qualified personnel can be obtained from:

- The General Council and Register of Osteopaths, 1–4 Suffolk Street, London SW1Y 4HG. Tel: 01–839 2060.
- British Chiropractic Association, 5 First Avenue, Chelmsford, Essex CM1 1RX. Tel: 0245 353078.

Property deals

Those who own or are considering buying a house or flat will probably need the services of various professionals such as estate agents, surveyors, valuers or perhaps architects or builders. Rights against solicitors and licensed conveyancers have been dealt with on pp. 81 and 85. What rights do consumers have against other service persons concerned with property deals?

Rights to sue for breach of contract, negligence or breach of statutory duty

If a consumer employs someone to survey or value a house which s/he intends to buy, or to design or build something, and the person employed does not exercise the degree of care and skill which could be reasonably expected then the consumer may well be able to sue for breach of contract or negligence. As will be explained later, there are time limits within which legal actions must be started and this could pose problems in property cases because a consumer may not realize for some time that a building job has not been done properly. So act quickly, as soon as you suspect there is something wrong, and immediately take advice.

In addition, there is a statute which imposes a duty in respect of building works. A service person who broke this duty would not be prosecuted in the criminal courts but could be sued for damages in the civil courts. The statute in question is the Defective Premises Act 1972 and in Section 1 it states that builders, subcontractors, architects and others must ensure that building work is done properly, with adequate materials and that as regards that work the dwelling will be fit for habitation when completed. In Northern Ireland this is covered by the Defective Premises (N1) Order 1975. In Scotland there is a duty implied by case law that a dwelling house must be fit for human habitation. In England and Wales also note that Section 38 of the Building Act 1984 will, when in force, provide that breach of a duty imposed by building regulations is to be actionable.

■ A would-be house purchaser arranged for a house to be surveyed. The surveyor's report stated that the house had been checked for damp with a protimeter and that there had been no reading of dampness. Later, after the house had been bought, it was discovered that in fact there was a serious damp problem due to a defective pipe which was leaking in two places. The judge decided that this evidence of dampness would have been discovered if the protimeter had been more extensively used. The house had not been checked thoroughly enough. It was the duty of the surveyor to exercise that degree of care and skill which a reasonably competent surveyor would exercise. The surveyor was ordered to pay damages for redecoration, reduced value of carpets, inconvenience and distress. (Fryer v Bunney (1982) 263 EG 158)

Architects

If you employ an architect that person will usually be responsible for matters of design, planning permission and for protecting your interests with regard to any builders also employed. Anyone can do this sort of work but it is a criminal offence under the Architects Registration Act for a person to describe him/herself as being an architect unless s/he is qualified as such and registered with the Architects Registration Council. The only persons who can do this kind of work without being qualified as architects are properly qualified engineers or surveyors.

The same Act obliges the Architects Registration Council to discipline errant architects, who can be struck off the register following the commission of a criminal offence or for conduct disgraceful to their capacity as an architect. The Council also publishes a Standard of Conduct which includes the statement that an architect 'will assure himself that information given in connection with his services is in substance and presentation factual and relevant to the occasion and neither misleading nor unfair to others . . .' Architects should also before entering into deals with clients 'have defined beyond all reasonable doubt the terms of the engagement including the scope of the service, the allocation of responsibilities and any limitation of liability, the method of calculation of remuneration and the provision for termination'. The Council may call an architect to account for failing to adhere to the provisions of the Standard of Conduct. When agreeing the deal many architects will use a standard form of contract drawn up by, for example, the Royal Institute of British Architects (an architects' pressure group to which many belong). Do read this contract carefully before agreeing to sign it.

If you want to complain about an architect the address of the Architects Registration Council is 73 Hallam Street, London W1N 6EE.

Estate agents

Anyone can set themselves up as an estate agent but the operations of such persons are now controlled by the Estate Agents Act 1979. Breach of the rules set down by this Act can result in an estate agent being prosecuted in the criminal courts or being banned from the business of estate agency by the Director General of Fair Trading. The Director can also formally warn estate agents and the fact that an estate agent had already been warned would be taken into account when deciding whether to prohibit them from trading following any further transgressions.

The Act provides that estate agents must tell consumers if they have some personal interest in the property being dealt with. They may not, for example, arrange the sale of your house at a very cheap price to, say, a company who is really just their nominee without telling you of the connection. Contravention of this provision can lead to a warning.

There is no law that says you must give an estate agent a pre-contract deposit and in Scotland this is banned altogether. However, any money given to an estate agent as a pre-contract or contractual deposit must be paid into a separate client account and proper accounts must be kept. If this is not done or the estate agent runs off with the money then s/he can be prosecuted in the criminal courts, warned or banned altogether. If the estate agent holds more than £500 (except as a 'stakeholder', a conveyancing term which there is not room to explain – seek advice) and this money would in normal circumstances attract interest of more than £10 then s/he must give that amount of interest to the customer.

Section 18 of the Act states that estate agents must make clear how much money the customer is to be charged and in what circumstances. If the estate agent fails to clarify this important point and then later attempts to sue a customer for fees, the court has the power to deprive the estate agent of all the money if it considers that it would be just to do so. Estate agents can also be banned or warned for contravening this provision.

Some estate agents belong to the National Association of Estate Agents, Arbon House, 21 Jury Street, Warwick CV34 4EH. Tel:

0906 496800. This Association has drawn up Rules of Conduct and will reprimand, fine, suspend or expel members who do not adhere to the Rules. Members must not, for example, perform any act which involves dishonesty, dishonourable or deceitful behaviour or which is unfair to members of the public. Members also must not propose terms to a prospective client which are otherwise than fair or reasonable.

Surveyors

There is no specific statutory control over surveyors, but if they act as estate agents then they are liable to control under the above mentioned Estate Agents Act 1979.

The Royal Institution of Chartered Surveyors (12 Great George Street, Parliament Square, London SW1P 3AD. Tel: 01–222 7000) will investigate certain types of complaint about surveyors who are members of the Institution. They will *not* investigate complaints about the levels of fees charged nor will they investigate accusations of negligence. They will look into allegations of delay, failure to answer letters, wrongful disclosure of confidential information, failure to disclose any conflict of interest between surveyor and client and failure to deal properly with money entrusted to the surveyor.

Many consumers come into contact with surveyors or valuers when intending to buy a property on mortgage. In such situations building societies send in their own valuer and then charge the consumer a fee for that person's services. In one well-publicized case* the purchasers successfully sued the building society surveyor for negligence even though they had not directly employed the surveyor themselves. This is possible in negligence claims. However in a recent case** where a building society used an exclusion clause in their application form disclaiming responsibility for errors in their valuer's report, the court allowed them to use this clause to avoid paying damages to a purchaser. The court decided the clause was not unreasonable under the Unfair Contract Terms Act (see p. 70). If you plan to buy a house on mortgage, it might be best to get a report of your own if you can afford to do so.

---

* Yianni v Edwin Evans and Sons (1982) 1 QB 438.
** Stevenson v Nationwide Building Society (1984) 272 EG 663.

Builders

If you have decided to have building work done and to dispense with the services of an architect or surveyor then you should be particularly careful. Numerous pitfalls await the unwary. Do you know whether you need planning permission, for example? How good is your knowledge of the Building Regulations? Violation of either could land you in trouble. In addition sob stories abound on the subject of building jobs that went on and on costing more and more, roofs that leaked the first time it rained, etc., etc. As far as the law is concerned, anyone can set up as a builder and although you can in theory sue if things go wrong, this will be of no use if the offender later disappears or goes out of business. With careful forethought, however, consumers can do much to protect their own interests.

We emphasize again the need for a written contract. This should deal with the likely problems mentioned above (and see p. 68). The August 1985 edition of *Which?* magazine contains on p. 359 a sample contract and many other handy hints on the subject of builders.

Some builders have chosen to join trade associations. A consumer who deals with one such will be better protected, particularly as guarantee schemes are on offer which ensure some level of redress if things go wrong. Builders who have joined the Building Employers Federation, for example, can offer customers the benefit of a guarantee scheme operated by the BEC Building Trust Ltd. The scheme covers works costing between £500 and £25,000 where there is no supervision by an architect or surveyor. The customer has to sign a scheme building agreement, pay a fee of one per cent of the contract price (minimum £20) and sign an application to register this. Later the customer receives a registration certificate from the Trust. The Trust then guarantees that the member will finish the job properly, will remedy any defects that appear within six months and will also remedy any structural defects that appear within two years, provided they arise in the foundations or load-bearing part of a roof, floor or wall and are the fault of the member. If the member goes out of business the Trust will get another member to finish any job started, but will only pay up to £5,000 for any extra costs thus incurred. The Trust offers an arbitration scheme and will honour any arbitration award not honoured by a member, but once again only up to a maximum of £5,000. If you go to arbitration you cannot also go to court, so take advice before deciding. The Trust is at Invicta House, London Road, Maidstone, Kent ME16 8JH. Tel: 0622 683791. You can find out from them which local builders are members. Other trading associations are the Federation of Master Builders, 33 John Street, London WC1N 2BB, and the Scottish Building Employers Federation, 13 Woodside Crescent, Glasgow G3 7UP.

Additionally, if you are thinking of buying a new house or one that is less than 10 years old, there is another guarantee scheme of which you should be able to take advantage. The National House Building Council (NHBC) (Portland Place, London W1N 4BU. Tel: 01–637 1248/9) operates a scheme whereby builders registered with them (and they will remove builders from the list for bad behaviour) undertake to remedy certain (not all) defects which might occur within 10 years of construction. The benefit of the policy can be passed on to subsequent purchasers. If you are thinking of buying a new or under ten-year-old house always ask first if there is an NHBC agreement and if not, why not.

Double-glazing

Consumers are frequently encouraged to invest in double-glazing, and complaints that occur following dissatisfaction with such installations demand attention. Apart from the rights to sue set out above, the key to not being cheated in this area may well lie in whom you deal with.

Some glaziers are members of the Glass Federation, 6 Mount Row, London W1Y 6DY. Tel: 01–409 0545. Membership is not compulsory and no particular qualifications are required by statute before a person is permitted to do glazing work. The Federation has, however, drawn up a code of practice in consultation with the Office of Fair Trading and it is a condition of membership that the entirety of the code be accepted. A member who breaches the Code can be reprimanded or expelled. The following are important provisions of the Code:

- Customers who sign cash deals off business premises, e.g. at home, must be permitted to cancel them within five days. This is worth noting because the law only provides similar protective 'cooling off' periods for credit deals.
- It is customary for a deposit to be required before work begins. If a firm who takes a deposit later goes out of

business the consumer would normally have little redress. However, the Federation guarantees that if one of their members goes bust after receiving a deposit they will either ensure the work is done at a fair market price, credit being given for the deposit, or they will refund the money. *But* only contracts valued at less than £6,000 are covered and only up to 25 per cent of a deposit on a 'supply and fixing' contract and up to 50 per cent of a deposit of a deposit on a 'supply only' contract will be refunded or credited.

- Materials supplied and work done must be up to standards set by the Federation and the British Standards Institution.
- The contract with the customer must include a clause dealing with cancellation in the event of delay.
- Any complaints that cannot be settled between customer and glazier can be referred to the Federation. If that does not work then, as an alternative to court proceedings (you cannot do both), the Federation offers low cost arbitration.

Other relevant tradespersons

There is no statutory control over who can set themselves up as a electricians, plumbers, etc. At present only the glaziers have agreed a specific code of practice with the Office of Fair Trading. However, there are trading associations to which other relevant tradespersons might belong. The Office of Fair Trading publishes a leaflet called *Home Improvements* which has details.

6.

Financial services

Insurance

Some people feel that insurance companies are quick to take a customer's money but slow to pay up in the event of a claim. Below we deal with points to look out for when agreeing to take out an insurance policy or when making a claim. There are some unusual legal rules that apply to insurance deals, but various codes of practice have been drawn up which could on a voluntary basis mitigate the harsh effect of these legal rules. Most insurance companies, for instance, belong to the Association of British Insurers (ABI), which has a code regarding insurance practices. The ABI states that it 'can often help to clear up misunderstandings between insurance companies and members of the public'. Consumers who cannot sort out such 'misunderstandings' with their insurance company can contact the ABI's Consumer Information Department or complain to the Insurance ombudsman. The address of the ABI is Aldermary House, Queen Street, London EC4N 1TT. Tel: 01–248 4477.

Agreeing the deal

Most provisions of the Unfair Contract Terms Act 1977 do not apply to insurance companies (see p. 70).

When signing an insurance contract you are under a legal duty voluntarily to disclose any fact that might influence the insurance company's estimate of the degree of risk involved. This applies even if they do not ask you about the fact in question. If you do not reveal something relevant, the insurance company is entitled to invalidate your agreement with them but they are unlikely to bother until you make a claim! You also must reveal any important new facts each time you renew your policy. Not surprisingly, it has been suggested that this rule, which is based on decided court cases, is somewhat unfair.

■ In April 1963 a woman signed an 'all risks' insurance proposal form to cover jewellery belonging to herself and her husband. She was not asked whether either of them had a criminal record. She knew that some years previously her husband had been found guilty of the crime of receiving 1,730 stolen cigarettes for which he was fined £25. Not surprisingly, she did not volunteer information about this event to the insurance company. The policy was renewed from year to year, the last renewal being in March 1972. In December 1971 the husband had received a 15–month prison sentence for offences of dishonesty. In April 1972 the wife claimed under the policy £311 for seven items of jewellery lost or stolen.

The court held she could not claim. Not only should she have told the insurance company about the cigarette conviction when originally signing the proposal form, but she should also have told them when renewing the policy in March 1972 about her husband's second conviction. (Lambert v Co-operative Insurance Society Ltd (1975) 2 Lloyds Rep. 485).

The ABI's statement of practice now provides that a member company's proposal forms must warn people of the consequences of failure to disclose all material facts and direct them when in doubt to reveal all. Also, proposal forms should ask clear questions about those facts which usually are material, e.g. criminal records. Renewal notices should warn of the need to reveal new material facts. The law is still the law though, so when filling out the form make sure you have disclosed everything that might be relevant to the deal.

It is also important not to make any mistakes in your answers. If you do your claim could be later disallowed even if the mistake was not deliberate. The ABI code states that people should only be required to certify that their answers are correct according to their knowledge and belief. Also, people should not be asked questions which only experts could answer or which involve making a value judgement.

Make sure you are not underinsured. If the item insured has increased in value and you have not told the insurance company, you may be able to recover only part of its value if it is lost or destroyed. Read what your policy says about this carefully. If the phrase 'subject to average' is used, for example, then the rules about underinsurance do apply.

You must have what is called an 'insurable interest' in what is being insured. This means that you personally will lose out if the event insured against takes place. You cannot, for example, insure jewellery against theft if you do not own it.

A person may not take out two insurance policies against the same event and then claim double the money in the event of a loss. By law, you can only get in total what the loss is worth and the insurance companies will probably divide the expense between them.

Insurance claims

First read the policy and see what you agreed to do in the event of a loss. The ABI's code states that you should only be asked to report a claim and subsequent developments as soon as possible. Make sure you keep to what you agreed because failure to use the correct claims procedure might lead to your claim being disallowed. Take advice if this happens; they might not be able to get away with it but the law is complicated.

Your claim might also be disallowed because of non-disclosure or misrepresentation. Failure to comply with other terms of the policy could also lead to a claim being disallowed. The ABI code states that a claim should not be disallowed on these bases if the non-disclosure was not important or the breach of term irrelevant to the loss unless there has been fraud, deception or negligence.

In the case of a car accident you may have a choice of insurance companies to claim against: the other person's if it was his/her fault, or your own. Make sure you claim against the other person whenever possible, otherwise you could lose your no-claims bonus. Make the fact that you are claiming against the other person clear to your own insurance company. If you later successfully get the other person to pay, your own no-claims bonus should not be affected even if the insurance companies do have an administratively convenient arrangement (called 'knock-for-knock') going. If you belong to the AA or RAC you can ask them for advice.

If a claim is disallowed unfairly or there is delay in paying you, it is worth complaining to the ABI or insurance ombudsman (see below). The ABI code says there should be no delay in paying agreed claims. Your official legal remedy would be to sue for breach of the insurance contract, but take advice first as this is not an easy area of law.

Statutory protection

There are various statutory controls over the insurance business, including the following:

- Only properly authorised bodies are allowed to carry on the business of insurance and there are controls over advertisements. Persons who carry out insurance business without being authorized or who make false, deceptive, dishonest or reckless promises or forecasts so as to induce another person to enter into an insurance deal can be prosecuted in the criminal courts.
- It is also a criminal offence to describe oneself as an 'insurance broker' without being registered with the Insurance Brokers Registration Council. The Council has drawn up a code of conduct and will de-register badly behaved insurance brokers. They state that they will deal with complaints made about registered insurance brokers by members of the public. Their address is 15 St Helens Place, London EC3A 6DS. Tel: 01–588 4387. The ABI has also drawn up a non-statutory code of practice for member intermediaries who are not registered insurance brokers.
- If an insurance company goes out of business then a consumer can still obtain 90 per cent of the benefits s/he would have entitled to under the policy (100 per cent in the case of compulsory, e.g. third party car, insurance). This protection is provided by the Policy Holders Protection Act 1975 which obliges all insurance companies to fund a scheme to compensate policy holders in the event of an insurance company getting into insuperable difficulties. Insurance brokers must insure against claims being made against them.
- If you are injured in a road accident by a driver who is not insured, whose insurance is dishonoured for some reason or who disappears without trace then all is not lost. A body called the Motor Insurers Bureau (also funded by insurance companies) is obliged to compensate victims in such circumstances if certain criteria are met. The criteria include an obligation to notify the Bureau before issuing any legal proceedings. It is probably best to take advice in such

circumstances. (Note that the scheme only covers injuries, not damage to property.)

- Under the Insurance Companies Act 1982 consumers who sign proposal forms for some types of life insurance policies are given an opportunity to get out of the deal later after a period of reflection. The insurance company must send consumers a notice drawing their attention to the need to consider the terms of the policy carefully and also telling them of their right to withdraw within 10 days of receiving the notice. (Certain types of policy are not covered by these provisions, e.g. contracts under which the benefits payable are secured by the payment of a single premium.)

The insurance ombudsman

This position was created on a voluntary basis after a series of complaints about bad behaviour by insurance companies. If the company you are insured with has chosen to be a member of the scheme then you can complain about it to the Insurance Ombudsman, The Insurance Ombudsman Bureau, 31 Southampton Row, London WC1B 5HJ. Tel: 01–242 8613. You must complain within six months of the final decision by your insurance company about which you are complaining. The ombudsman will investigate such matters as not being offered enough when claiming, not getting anything when claiming, or delay in settling a claim. If the ombudsman makes a decision in your favour and you accept that decision then your insurance company must pay the awarded amount to a maximum of £100,000. If you do not accept the decision you still can go to court over it. Note that the ombudsman will not be prepared to investigate anything which is currently the subject of litigation.

Banks

Most of us have a bank account. The relationship consumers have with their banks may or may not be a happy one. Below we set out what duties your bank owes to you and those you owe to it.

Bouncing cheques

If you write out a cheque to someone and either have sufficient funds in your current account or an agreed overdraft arrangement to cover the amount, then the bank has no right to dishonour it. If a bank wrongly bounces your cheque then you can sue them for damage to your reputation.

Stolen cheques and forgeries

A bank has a duty to know what their customers' signatures look like, but a customer is under a duty not to facilitate fraud. If you make out a cheque in such a way as to make fraud easy you might lose out. Signing a blank cheque is an obvious example of this. If you do this and the cheque is misused then your bank might be within its rights to refuse to refund the money that is thereby removed from your bank account. If your cheque book is stolen or for some other reason your signature is forged, then the cheque is a nullity and the bank cannot debit your account. However, if you know that a forged cheque might be presented and do not warn the bank, they might be within their rights to refuse to refund you.

Cheque cards

These are a guarantee by the bank to the person you write a cheque to that the bank will pay the amount up to (at present) £50. The bank will therefore, provided the cheque is written out correctly, honour it even if you do not have that amount of money in the account. However, deliberate and dishonest misuse of a cheque card to obtain unauthorized credit could result in criminal prosecution. If your card is stolen make sure you tell your bank without delay.

Bank cash till cards

These are very convenient but can cause problems. It is not easy to argue with a computer which says someone used your secret number to withdraw cash even though you know this did not happen or if it did it was not your fault. It is important therefore to keep your cash till receipts and check them against monthly bank statements. That way if there is a computer malfunction you will hopefully spot it at an early stage. If the bank will not then refund your money, consider a complaint to the ombudsman (see later). Also note that a bank cash till card might attract the control of the Consumer Credit Act if a customer was allowed to use it to overdraw (see p. 153).

Credit cards

Credit cards are dealt with on p. 145.

Advice by your bank

If your bank offers you advice about such matters as investments or undertakes accountancy or probate work for you then, like any other professional adviser, they are under a duty to act competently and can be sued for negligence if they do not do so.

Statutory protection

The business of banking is to some extent now controlled by the

Banking Act 1979. Consumers might like to know that some money in a deposit fund will be refunded if a bank or other licensed institution goes out of business. You get 75 per cent of what was in there up to a maximum of £10,000.

The banking ombudsman

The banking ombudsman will deal with complaints about the provision in the UK of banking services by any member bank to any individual. The ombudsman will attempt to get the matter sorted out satisfactorily and can make awards of compensation of up to £50,000 which the bank must honour. Note the following:

- The complaint to the ombudsman must be made within six months of the last word on the subject by the bank in question.
- The incident must not have occurred more than 6 years ago. (The right to sue in court would also be lost by that time.)
- The incident must have occurred on or after 1 January 1986 or the consumer must not (with reasonable grounds) have found out about it until after that date.
- If you do decide to accept any offer of compensation made via the ombudsman you will thereby lose your right to sue in court over the matter. If in any doubt therefore as to whether any offer made is sufficient, take advice before accepting it.

The banking ombudsman is Mr Ian Edwards-Jones QC, Citadel House, 5–11 Fetter Lane, London EC4A 1BR.

Accountants

Most consumers who come across accountants do so in the context of their tax affairs, but the latter are prepared to advise on a wide range of financial matters. There is no law that says that a person who helps you with your tax return has to be qualified. However, official audits of companies and charities etc. must be signed by properly qualified persons.

If accountants do not do the work you ask them to do to a reasonable standard you can sue them for breach of contract or negligence as with any other professional adviser. Complaints about bad behaviour by an accountant who is a member of the Institute of Chartered Accountants can be made to the Institute at PO Box 433, Chartered Accountants Hall, Moorgate Place, London EC2P 2BJ. Tel: 01–628 7060. (Scotland and Northern Ireland have separate organizations.) The Institute will investigate allegations of misconduct such as lack of integrity, breach of confidentiality, bad or no service, but they will not look into a complaint that an accountant's bill is too high. They do, however, advise their members that their bills should enable a client to identify what work has been carried out and will arrange arbitration if required to do so. However, the arbitrator will charge a fee apportioned, at his discretion, between the parties. Members who are found guilty of misconduct can be expelled from membership, fined or reprimanded. Bad behaviour by an accountant which is sufficiently serious to give rise to public concern would be referred to a Joint Disciplinary Committee.

Stockbrokers

Dealers in securities must either be licensed by the government or else belong to a recognized institution such as the Stock Exchange. It is a criminal offence to make false, misleading or deceptive statements to persuade a person to buy securities. The government can investigate the administration of a unit trust if such an investigation would be in the interests of the unit holders and the matter is one of public concern.

Licensed dealers must comply with generally accepted standards of good market practice and if they behave badly they can lose their licence. Members of the Stock Exchange can be expelled or reprimanded for conduct which is dishonourable or disgraceful, improper or unbecoming the character of a member.

The government intends to reform the law in this area so that better and more comprehensive protection can be given to would-be investors.

7.

Major service industries

Some major service industries have been taken into public ownership and despite the much vaunted plans to sell all of them off it is unlikely that consumers will face any less of a monopoly situation in that event than they do at present.

In this section we deal with a consumers rights vis a vis the Post Office, British Telecom, and the electricity gas and transport industries. We also deal with the government ombudsmen schemes whereby complaints can be made against publicly funded bodies.

The Post Office

The powers and duties of the Post Office are controlled by statute. Section 59 of the British Telecommunications Act 1981 imposes a general duty on the Post Office to satisfy so far as is reasonably practicable (and so long as no one else is providing the service) all reasonable demands made for services in the British Isles for the conveyance of letters.

The Unfair Contract Terms Act 1977 does not apply to the Post Office (see p. 69). The Post Office also enjoys a general immunity against being sued in the courts for loss or damage caused by their acts or omissions. The Post Office can be sued if a registered inland packet is lost but there is a maximum limit to the compensation that can be awarded and the legal proceedings must be started within 12 months of the loss. This is a shorter time limit than usual (see p. 20). Losers of such packets can also claim under the following compensation scheme.

The Post Office has a compensation scheme in relation to loss or damage to things sent through the post.

- *Ordinary post.* You are supposed to have got a certificate of posting (but failure to have done so is not fatal). You will get only the market value of the object lost or loss of value in the case of damage and only up to a maximum of, at present, £16.50.

- *Recorded delivery*. A maximum £18 can be awarded. You will have been given a receipt automatically, whereas with ordinary post you would have to ask for one. You should not use recorded delivery or ordinary post for sending money or articles of value.
- *Registered letter*. You can be compensated according to how much money you paid, up to a maximum of £1,500.
- *Compensation Fee Parcel Service*. Once again you can obtain compensation according to the fee paid, up to a maximum of £300.

To apply for compensation, fill in a form at any post office. There is a 12-month time limit.

If you want to complain about the offer made under the compensation scheme or about anything else you should write to your local head postmaster. If you are not satisfied with the reply you can complain further to the Regional Director. Complaints can also be made to the Post Office Users National Council, which has separate offices for England, Wales, Scotland and Northern Ireland (addresses in phone book). Dissatisfied claimants of compensation can go to arbitration instead of going to court. Complaints about maladministration by the Post Office can be referred to the ombudsman. (See p. 113).

It is a criminal offence to post dangerous or obscene material.

Telephone services

This industry is now in private hands, the machinery for denationalization being provided by the Telecommunications Act 1984. Under the Act there is an Office of Telecommunications headed by a Director General of Telecommunications headed by a Director General of Telecommunications who licenses those wishing to operate in the business. The Director is obliged by the statute to ensure that all reasonable demands for phone services are met, in particular, emergency services, public call box services, directory information services, and services in rural areas. The Director is also legally obliged to protect consumers' interests in respect of telephone services and prices. This duty is owed to all consumers but particularly to pensioners and the disabled.

The Director must look into any complaint made to him/her about telephone services. To this end Advisory Committees on Telecommunications have been established in England, Scotland, Wales and Northern Ireland. The Director must also encourage the adoption of voluntary codes of practice by those with licences. British Telecom has published such a code in consultation with the Office of Fair Trading. Under the code, British Telecom states that they will attempt to install a new phone within three to four weeks of being asked and they say most faults will be repaired within two days (a reduction of rental is offered if not). Complaints can be made to British Telecom itself who offer arbitration as an alternative to court proceedings or to the Advisory Committees on Telecommunications.

Electricity services

In 1947 the industry of supplying electricity was nationalized. In England and Wales (there are separate organizations for Scotland and Northern Ireland) the Central Electricity Generating Board generates electricity which it then sells to the various area electricity boards. The latter are under a statutory duty to plan and carry out efficient and economical distribution of electricity supplies to those who require them. Each area board has a consultative council, whose address you should be able to find on the back of your bill. The consultative council is supposed to represent the consumer point of view to the area board and will also investigate consumer complaints provided the board have first been given a chance to sort the matter out. There is in addition an Electricity Consumer's Council which represents consumers' interests at national level, and a central policy-making body called the Electricity Council.

There are various legal rights in relation to electricity. For example, any person 50 yards from a distributing main which is already supplying electricity to private consumers may demand a supply, although lines more than 60 feet from the main or on your own property must be paid for by you. If you are renting premises your landlord is allowed to resell electricity to you but the local area board will tell you the maximum price the landlord is permitted to charge. You can sue in the civil courts if you have been overcharged and recover the excess. If you are threatened with being cut off because the landlord has not paid the bill, contact your local authority and they can assist in arranging for you to pay direct. According to the Electricity Code of Practice (see below) the Board will delay cutting off tenants for 14 days while this is being sorted out. You cannot be asked to pay for a previous occupant's bill but when you leave yourself you must give 24 hours' written notice to avoid being charged for electricity used after you left.

A code of practice issued by both the electricity and gas (see later) industries states that consumers who get into difficulties with their bills will not be cut off if they make and keep to an arrangement to pay off the arrears in instalments. Also, old age pensioners will not be cut off between 1 October and 31 March if they cannot afford to pay the bill. A consumer will not be cut off if it is possible to install a slot meter which will be set so that the debt is collected as well as current electricity being paid for.

If the Electricity Board do want to cut off a consumer then they cannot enter his/her home for this purpose without obtaining either the consumer's consent or a court warrant. Before the warrant is issued the consumer must be warned of the intended entry.

Gas services

The industry of supplying gas was nationalized in 1949. The Gas Act 1972 established the British Gas Corporation which is under a duty to develop and maintain an efficient, co-ordinated and economical system of gas supply for Great Britain and to satisfy so far as it is economical to do so all reasonable demands for gas in Great Britain. In general no one else may supply gas without the consent of the Corporation. The Corporation must supply gas on being asked to do so by an owner or occupier whose premises are not more than 25 yards away from a main through which gas is being distributed already, but the Corporation is excused from this obligation in certain circumstances, e.g. when the customer has not paid a previous bill. In Northern Ireland the industry remains in private hands. Recently the Gas (Northern Ireland) Order 1985 provided that gas undertakers no longer have legal obligations to supply gas but the Department of Economic Development must provide a scheme for financial assistance to consumers who lose their gas supply.

The Gas Act 1972 also established a national and various regional gas consumers councils. The address of your local council should be on the back of your bill if you want to complain about something. The councils are under a duty to consider matters affecting the interests of consumers in their area whether or not the particular issue has been the subject of a complaint. In particular, they must consider issues relating to the supply of gas, gas fittings, services and gas charges. The National Council considers matters that relate to consumers throughout the country whether or not such issues are referred to them by the regional councils.

The Gas Board adopts the same code of practice regarding payment of bills as the Electricity Board (see above). Before cutting you off the Gas Board must also wait for 28 days after sending the bill and then give at least 7 days' notice of any intended cut-off. The necessity to obtain a warrant to enter a consumer's home without consent and the rules about resale of gas by landlords are also the same as for electricity.

There are a number of rules regarding gas safety. The Gas Act gives the government the right to make regulations regarding gas safety. Anyone who disobeys these provisions can be prosecuted in the criminal courts. For example, it is an offence to install a gas appliance which does not remove the products of combustion adequately or which does not have an adequate supply of air. It is also an offence to install a gas appliance without being competent to do so. The Gas Board recommends that consumers should use either Gas Board plumbers or those who belong to the Confederation for the Registration of Installers (CORGI). Its headquarters are at St Martins House, 140 Tottenham Court Road, London W1P 9LN. It is also an offence not to turn the gas off if you suspect a leak.

British Gas are under a duty to prevent gas escaping immediately they receive written notice of a leak and if they do not effactually prevent gas escape within 24 hours of getting the notice they can be prosecuted.

Transport services

Transport services are owned by a variety of private municipal and nationalized concerns. When consumers travel on a bus or train they enter into a contract with the organization in question under which the traveller has the right to arrive safely at the other end. It is likely that the organization will want to control the terms of the 'contract' by referring to their standard conditions. The court will strike out particularly unfair terms under the Unfair Contract Terms Act (see case on p. 70). Transport organizations can be prosecuted like any other service business for making false statements.

Under the Transport Act 1985 local authorities in England, Wales and Scotland have a duty to secure the provision of such public passenger transport services as they consider appropriate to meet any public transport requirements which in their opinion would not be met in any other way.

British Rail has a statutory responsibility under the Transport Act 1962 to provide railway services with due regard to efficiency and safety. Also established by the statute on a regional basis are Transport Users Consultative Committees which have a duty to consider any matter concerning the services and facilities provided by British Rail and concerning which users have made representations. There is also a Central Transport Consultative Committee in conjunction with which British Rail has drawn up a code of practice which British Rail say can be looked at at any manned British Rail station or rail appointed travel agency. The code deals with ticket refunds and lost tickets, and there is also a procedure for complaints and compensation claims. Except for ticket refunds, where passengers fill out a form at ticket offices or travel agents, write first to the local area manager whose address and phone number should be prominently displayed at stations and who should reply within five working days. If not satisfied with the answer, passengers can then refer the matter to their local Transport Users Consultative Committee (London Regional Passenger Committee in London). The address and phone number should be exhibited on notices at stations. In the case of compensation claims there is, as a last resort, the chance to opt for arbitration instead of going to court, for claims of less than £500 which do not relate to personal injury. But passengers wanting arbitration must apply for it within three months of receiving the last substantive reply from British Rail.

Some local authorities have established committees to look into complaints about their bus services. Also the Bus and Coach Council (see p. 118 for address) to which 98 per cent of all buses and 70 per cent of all coach services, whether publicly or privately owned, belong will consider serious complaints, e.g. about safety matters, and will encourage their members to look into less serious allegagions about operational problems such as late arrival.

The Civil Aviation Act obliges the Civil Aviation Authority (CAA) to ensure that British airlines provide air transport services which satisfy all substantial categories of public demand so far as it is reasonable. They should do this at the lowest charges possible consistent with a high standard of safety and an economic return to efficient operators. The CAA must also further the reasonable interests of users and the Air Transport Users Committee (129 Kingsway, London WC2A 6NN) has been set up to make recommendations to the CAA on this subject. Its duties include investigating complaints against airlines. Each major airport has an Airport Consultative Committee which deals with complaints relating to airport facilities or the lack of them. Some airlines also have their own voluntary consumer complaints procedure. The Carriage by Air Act 1961 provides that airlines must pay compensation up to certain limits following death or injury to a passenger, loss or damage to baggage or cargo and for delay. The airlines can escape liability in certain circumstances where economic claims only are involved. Note too that the obligation (see p. 117) for air travel organizers to be licensed when selling chartered air seats applies even if a holiday is not also being sold. The sale of scheduled airline seats is not covered by the bonding scheme.

Government ombudsmen schemes

The Health Service ombudsman has already been mentioned (see p. 90), and there are two other sorts of ombudsman established by statute. The Parliamentary Commissioner for Administration investigates complaints made about injustice suffered as a result of maladministration by certain government departments and authorities, e.g. the Post Office and the Office of Fair Trading. The commissioners for local administration investigate the same sorts of complaints when made against local and other authorities, e.g. water authorities.

The government ombudsmen will not investigate a complaint if the aggrieved person could take the matter to a tribunal or court unless the ombudsman feels it would be unreasonable for them to have to do so. The consumer must complain within 12 months of knowing about the matter complained of. (There is a discretion to consider late complaints but do not risk it.) A complaint to the Parliamentary Commissioner must be referred to him/her by an MP so you must write to an MP first. A complaint to a local commissioner must be referred to him/her via the complained-about authority, or, if the consumer writes to the commissioner direct, s/he will want to have confirmation that the authority has been told of the complaint and been given a reasonable opportunity to investigate and reply. To start the process therefore, write to the authority and make it clear that you want the matter referred to the commissioner if they will not resolve it. If you hear nothing then write to the commissioner with a copy of the letter you sent to the authority.

If the commissioners decide not to investigate the complaint they must reply to the MP or the consumer explaining their decision. If they do investigate the matter then the inquiry will not be in public, but apart from that they will decide how to carry out the investigation. They can legally order persons to attend as witnesses and produce documents and the consumer can be awarded expenses for attending or providing information. The parliamentary ombudsman must give the MP a copy of his/her report and if s/he considers an injustice has been suffered which has not or will not be remedied s/he can present a special report to the House of Commons. Local commissioners must send complaining consumers a copy of their report and if they consider that there has been injustice the authority complained about must consider these findings and tell the commissioner what action they will take to put matters right. If the commissioner does not receive a satisfactory response from them, s/he will make a further report stating this fact.

8.

Services with codes of practice

In this section we will deal with services which have trade associations and codes of practice.

Cars and motorbikes

The codes of practice subscribed to by the trading associations referred to on p. 42 contain sections concerning repairs and servicing performed otherwise than under a manufacturer's guarantee. Under the codes manufacturers accept a responsibility for ensuring the availability of spare parts at the time a new model is released, throughout its production and for a reasonable time thereafter. Repairers are to provide a written quotation, giving a definite price which will not be exceeded, wherever possible. At the least, they are to provide an estimate (also in writing if the customer requests it) which they are not to exceed by a significant amount without the customer's permission. Repairs are to be guaranteed against a failure due to workmanship for a specific mileage or time period which is to be stated on the invoice. The same complaints procedure as is mentioned on p. 43 is available.

Note, too, that there is another relevant trade association with its own code of practice which will deal with complaints against members. That is the Vehicle Builders and Repairers Association Ltd, Belmont House, 102 Finkle Lane, Gildersome, Leeds LS27 7TW.

Furniture

The code of practice for furniture has already been mentioned on p. 44. The code provides that if a consumer has bought new furniture which later needs repairing then a code member must agree who is to pay for what before the work is begun. If retailers accept that the repair is their responsibility then they must pay for everything but in other cases the retailer can agree to share the costs with the customer.

Footwear

The two major trading associations to which shoe repairers may belong are the National Association of Multiple Shoe Repairers (60 Wickham Hill, Hurstpierpoint, Hassocks, Sussex BN6 9NP. Tel: 07918 3488) and the Society of Master Shoe Repairers. Both use the same code of practice which has been drawn up in consultation with the Office of Fair Trading. Members undertake, amongst other things, to provide customers with a ticket showing the cost of the repair requested and the estimated date of collection, to make every effort to ensure satisfaction of wear and workmanship and to correct defects in work or materials promptly or free of charge or to offer fair compensation. The associations operate a complaints procedure and members should provide full details of it in the event of an unresolved dispute.

Electric and electronic appliances

The code of practice drawn up by RETRA has already been mentioned on p. 45. Parts of that code deal with servicing and repairs to appliances and are broadly similar to provisions in the codes of practice drawn up by the Association of Manufacturers of Domestic Electrical Appliances (AMDEA House, 593 Hitchin Road, Stopsley, Luton LU2 7UN. Tel: 0582 412444) and by the Electricity Boards (see p. 109). Members of these organizations undertake whenever possible to make home visits within three working days of receiving a request for a home repair service. If a second visit is necessary it should usually take place within 15 working days. Eighty per cent of workshop repairs should be completed within five working days and the rest within 15 working days. Customers should be warned about any minimum charges. There are rules about how long spare parts should be available for. Repairs and parts are to be guaranteed for at least three months. The same complaints procedure is available as set out on p. 45.

Holidays

Holiday dissatisfaction has on occasion given rise to litigation in the courts (see p. 67). Another source of consumer misery has been sudden financial failure by tour operators leaving people stranded either abroad or at home minus a holiday that has been paid for in advance.

Some travel agents and tour operators are members of the Association of British Travel Agents (ABTA) (55–7 Newman Street, London W1P 4HA). ABTA has drawn up codes of practice for agents and operators, breach of which can lead to a fine, reprimand or expulsion from membership. The codes state that brochures must contain information that is clear and accurate. Tour operators should not cancel holidays except where really necessary but where they do so the customer is to be offered an alternative holiday or a refund. If material alterations (those caused by bad weather or strikes are not included) have to be made, clients who do not want to accept the alterations are to be offered a refund. If a hotel is overbooked and this is known before departure clients should be offered a refund or, if the overbooking is discovered too late, the customer must be accommodated elsewhere and given compensation if the alternative accommodation is inferior to that originally agreed on. Consumers must be informed as to when surcharges can be made and tour operators should only impose them for reasons beyond their control. Currency surcharges are not to be made during the last 30 days before a pre-booked holiday.

If a dispute between a customer and a ABTA member cannot be resolved, ABTA is prepared to conciliate and if that does not work there is an arbitration scheme. (Do not agree to this without advice as it may preclude your rights to go to court.)

Consumers who book a holiday through an ABTA agent and an ABTA tour operator are protected against financial collapse by either. If the holiday is in progress ABTA will try to ensure its continuance as planned and will return you to the UK. If the holiday has not yet begun, ABTA will either reimburse you, ensure the holiday goes ahead as planned or arrange another one. Note that both the agent you have booked with and the tour operator must be in ABTA to ensure this protection.

Anyone who offers travel to the public using charter air seats must have an Air Travel Organizers Licence (ATOL) from the Civil Aviation Authority. A licence will not be given unless a bonding arrangement is made. The latter will cover the cost in the event of a financial collapse by the operator, of ensuring that stranded passengers complete their holiday and return home, and that those who have paid for but not yet begun their holiday get a refund. Licensed organizers must display their ATOL number and, although travel agents acting on their behalf do not themselves need a licence, the CAA states that consumers should be told the name of the organizer whom they represent. Further information about ATOL can be obtained from the CAA, ATOL Section, 45–59 Kingsway, London WC2B 6TE. Tel: 01–379 7311, ex. 2687 or 2683.

Some coach operators are covered by bonding arrangements made by the Bus and Coach Council, Sardinia House, Lincoln's Inn Fields, London WC2. Tel: 01–831 7546. The protection offered is similar to the ABTA scheme so it is worth checking if your holiday would be covered.

If dissatisfied with a holiday you still have all the legal rights set out on p. 65. For other provisions regarding transport see p. 111 and for hotels see p. 120.

Cleaners

There have been various well-known court cases on the subject of dry cleaning, usually hinging on the extent to which cleaners can evade responsibility for damaged items by use of exclusion clauses. Now of course the Unfair Contract Terms Act (see p. 69) would only permit reliance on such a clause by cleaning firms if the clause was 'reasonable'. Cleaners can of course be sued for breach of contract (including breach of implied statutory terms) and negligence.

Some launderers and cleaners have chosen to join the Association of British Launderers and Cleaners (Lancaster Gate House, 319 Pinner Road, Harrow, Middlesex HA1 4HX. Tel: 01–863 7755).* They have thereby agreed to be bound by the Association's code of practice which has been drawn up in consultation with the Office of Fair Trading. The code does *not* cover services provided in launderettes and coin-operated dry cleaners. Under the code, members are to handle all items accepted by them for processing with care and, if asked to re-clean without charge something which due to their fault has not been cleaned properly. Members are to pay fair compensation for loss or damage due to their negligence and to reduce their price if an unreasonable delay has occurred in completing the job. Members who lose a customer's property through fire or burglary are to pay

---

* Also note the Ulster Launderers Association, c/o Lilliput Laundry, Dummurry. Tel: 618 353.

compensation (unless the customer has his/her own insurance). Complaints by customers are to be investigated promptly and if that does not resolve matters the association's Customer Advisory Service will try and conciliate. They may decide to send the article for testing at an independent establishment selected by the customer. If so, they may decide to pay for this themselves or they may ask the consumer to pay. In the latter event the consumer's money will be refunded if the complaint is upheld. The member must abide by any findings and the consumer is expected to, although legally there is nothing to stop the consumer taking the matter to court if unhappy with the result.

Funeral directors

The neccesity of dealing with such matters as funeral arrangements is one that most of us have to face at one time or another. It is at times of emotional upset that people are particularly vulnerable to exploitation.

Some funeral directors have joined the National Association of Funeral Directors (57 Doughty Street, London WC1N 2NE. Tel: 01–242 9388) and this association has drawn up a code of practice in consultation with the Office of Fair Trading. The code covers all services provided by members except the provision of gravestones. Members agree, amongst other things, to give a written estimate of their charges before the funeral takes place and to request authorization from the client before incurring any extra expenditure. Complaints about a member funeral director that cannot be resolved between the parties can be referred to the association for conciliation. Failing that, the association offers arbitration as an alternative to court proceedings. Take advice first as you cannot do both.

Photography

A code of practice called the 'Photocode' has been drawn up in consultation with the Office of Fair Trading. Various organizations belong, including those representing manufacturers and importers of film and equipment, retail pharmacists, film processors, repairers and photographers. The Photocode covers truth in advertisements and provides, amongst other things, transfer of equipment guarantees to new owners and extension of same by the amount of time the article spends under repair, and a 21-day normal period for repairs to be effected within. If a consumer is aggrieved by the behaviour of a Photocode member they can complain first to their trade association and if that does not resolve matters arbitration is offered. Take advice first as you cannot go to court if you agree to arbitration.

Hotels

There are certain unusual legal rules in relation to hotels, and any establishment which offers food, drink and accommodation to any traveller who appears able to pay and who is in a fit state to be received is covered by them. Such establishments must receive all travellers and, regardless of race or sex, entertain them at reasonable prices unless there are reasonable grounds for refusal, e.g. if the hotel is full or if the traveller turns up drunk. The hotel must also receive the traveller's car if it has the facilities to do so, and the traveller's luggage, providing it is not excessive. Hoteliers who wrongly refuse to admit someone can be sued for damages. Customers can lawfully be requested to pay in advance.

For historical reasons (i.e. the fact that innkeepers were once frequently in league with highwaymen) hotels are responsible for the safety of customers' possessions (excluding their car and anything in it) whilst these are in the hotel even if the disappearance is not because of something the hotel has done or failed to do. There are some exceptions to this rule. If the goods are lost through the fault of the guest, an act of God or of the Queen's enemies then the hotel is not liable to pay compensation. Hotels can also limit their liability to £50 per item or £100 overall per guest. The Hotel Proprietors Act 1956 (not applicable to Northern Ireland, although the Hotel Proprietors Act (NI) 1958 makes similar provisions) provides that the hotel must display a notice to that effect in a place where it can be conveniently read by guests. Hotels cannot use the notice to evade responsibility if goods are lost through their fault or if goods have been specifically deposited with the hotel for safe custody.

If you fail to pay the bill the hotel can keep your possessions with the exception of your vehicle, any property in it and your clothes. Under the Innkeepers Act 1878 the hotel can sell the retained possessions six weeks later, provided they have at least one month before the sale advertised it in a London and local newspaper.

Hiring things

Most of us hire something at one time or another, sometimes for short periods of time, e.g. a car for the weekend, and sometimes for much longer. A television, for example, might be rented for some years. The hired item still belongs legally to the person who hired it out and, the consumer has a duty to take reasonable care of it and can be forced to pay compensation if the item is damaged.

Hired goods must comply with their description and be of merchantable quality and fit for their required purpose. This is stated in Sections 8 and 9 of the Supply of Goods and Services Act 1982. * The provisions are phrased in the same way as those which cover the sale of goods so see pp. 16 and 29–33 for further explanation. Under the Unfair Contract Terms Act these provisions cannot be excluded against consumers. (See p. 69 for further explanation.)

Hiring agreements which are capable of lasting more than three months and where the total payments the consumer must make would not exceed £15,000 (£5,000 if the agreement was made before 20 May 1985) are controlled by the Consumer Credit Act 1974. The provisions of this Act are dealt with in the following chapters on credit and many of the controls imposed on credit bargains are the same as those imposed on hire agreements. These controls are briefly listed below with page references for the reader who requires further details.

- Persons who hire goods in circumstances where the Act applies must be licensed by the Director General of Fair Trading (see p. 128).
  The contents of hire advertisements are strictly controlled. Like HP advertisements (see p. 133), the advertisements are divided into categories and misleading hire advertisements are banned. Consumers wanting to hire something can request a hire quotation so they will know in advance such information as the amount of any requested advance payment and whether they will have to find a guarantor.
- There are strict rules about documentation, and if these are not adhered to the owner may not be able to enforce the

---

* This act does not apply in Scotland. There, the consumers would have to rely on the common law or Sale of Goods Act provisions, see p. 36.

agreement (see p. 134). The consumer has a right to cancellation after doorstep talk (see p. 129). Any person standing as guarantor has some protection (see p. 139).

- The consumer can ask for information whilst the agreement continues. Under Section 79 of the Act you can ask for a copy of the agreement and details of any money currently owing.
- If the consumer gets behind with payments a default notice must be served before the goods can be taken away (see p. 143). Owners are not allowed to force their way into consumers houses to take away the goods without a court order (see p. 143). You may decide to let them in if, you wish; if you no longer want the item this might save court costs. Consumers receiving a default notice can apply to the court for a time order (see p. 143).
- If the goods are snatched back without a court order or if the case is before the court and the court decides the goods must be returned (the court cannot delay the owner's right to have the goods returned), then the consumer can ask for a refund of money paid by him/her to the hirer. This is stated in Section 132 of the Consumer Credit Act. The court can grant this request if it considers it fair, given the length of time the consumer has had the goods.
- The consumer can terminate the agreement (whatever may be said to the contrary) after 18 months. This is stated in Section 101 of the Consumer Credit Act. The consumer must give written notice of three months or one payment period, whichever is the less, before doing so. This right to cancel applies to consumer but not to business hiring, and does not apply to hiring agreements where the yearly payments total more than £900.

Part III

Buying Credit

This section deals with the rights of the consumer when obtaining credit. Consumers may encounter all sorts of problems in this area, ranging from not being able to get any credit in the first place to not being able to pay off what has been borrowed. The Consumer Credit Act 1974 now regulates most of the credit agreements that consumers might enter into. The Act aims to ensure that people do not fall prey to over-persuasive doorstep salespersons or misleading advertisements. The contents of credit agreements are strictly controlled and consumers who get into financial difficulties are afforded some protection. Customers who buy goods on credit are sometimes able to sue not just the seller but also the credit provider if the goods are not satisfactory.

9.

Hire-purchase and conditional sale

Hire-purchase and conditional sale are convenient ways of obtaining something now and paying for it later by instalments. However, there are a number of disadvantages involved, the most obvious being the fact that the goods will in the end cost a lot more than if bought for cash. Below we deal with the most likely problems consumers may encounter, namely misinformation and no information, high-pressure doorstep selling, how to agree and get out of the deal and what to do if you cannot afford the repayments.

Technically a hire-purchase agreement is one whereby the buyer hires the goods from the seller, pays instalments and then becomes the owner of the goods once all the instalments are paid. A conditional sale occurs where a person simply agrees to buy goods by instalments but again does not become the owner until the payments have been completed. The important aspect of both types of deal is that the property remains legally the property of the lender until the deal is concluded. This means the consumer must take reasonable care of the property and must not sell it to anyone else. To save space we will just refer to hire-purchase from now on but the reader should take it that conditional sale is also included and that the position regarding both types of deal is the same unless we state otherwise.

The Consumer Credit Act regulates the business of hire purchase unless the total credit advanced exceeds £15,000 (£5,000 if the agreement was made before 20 May 1985). Calculating the credit element for this purpose is complicated so if you can afford HP facilities for an amount in that region and are not sure if your agreement is covered by the legislation then it is best to take advice. The rights set out in this section are based on the assumption that the HP agreement in question is within the limits of the legislation.

The Act provides that only persons granted a licence by the Director General of Fair Trading (see p. 175 for more details) may now conduct hire-purchase business. Anyone who does so without a licence commits a criminal offence and agreements made by an unlicensed person cannot be enforced against the customer unless and until the Director General directs otherwise. Only 'fit persons' should be given a licence and the Director can revoke or suspend a licence for bad behaviour. There is a register open to the public in which licence details can be inspected on payment of a fee at the Office of Fair Trading, Government Buildings, Bromyard Avenue, Acton, London W3 7BB (check opening times before going).

The following rules about misrepresentation and misdescription apply to both verbal and written contracts.

Sales talk

Misrepresentation

When buying goods on HP any conversations the consumer has obviously will usually be with the dealer or supplier. If those persons also provide the credit then the consumer has the same rights against them in respect of untrue or inaccurate statements made before the deal is struck as if paying by cash (see p. 15).

If, however, the person lending the money is someone else, such as a finance company, then the dealer will usually sell the goods to this company who will in turn let them out to the consumer. In such a situation Section 56 of the Consumer Credit Act provides that any representations made by shop persons to the customer are deemed to be made by them not just on their own behalf but also as agents of the lender. This means that if it is the finance company who is hiring the goods to the customer then that company can be sued if the dealer makes untruthful or inaccurate statements to the consumer before the sale.

■ A man went into some car showrooms and said that he was considering trading in his sports car in exchange for a car he could use as a minicab. He was shown a secondhand car by a salesman, the latter stating that the car had been a chauffeur-driven company car. (In fact its only previous owner, who had owned it for two years, had used it in the course of his car-hire business. Hardly the same thing!) The salesman added that the car had just been serviced and was in excellent mechanical condition. The man then traded in his own car in part exchange, entered into a hire-purchase agreement with a finance company to provide the balance of the purchase price and took delivery of the car. It then turned out that in addition to numerous minor defects there were defects in the left upper suspension swivel, the right front wheel bearing and in particular the power steering. The net result was that the vehicle was unroadworthy and not fit to be used as a minicab from the point of view of reliability and road safety.

The man successfully sued the finance company who had provided the credit. The court held that the incorrect statement made, namely that the car was in excellent mechanical condition in the context of its proposed use as a minicab, amounted to a serious breach of contract. The finance company were also legally responsible for what had occurred. (Porter v General Guarantee Corporation Ltd (1982) RTR 384)

Misdescription

Consumers buying hire-purchase goods have the same rights to be provided with goods that live up to their description as those afforded to cash purchasers under Section 13 of the Sale of Goods Act (see p. 16). That section does apply to conditional sales but not to hire-purchase goods, but Section 9 of the Supply of Goods (Implied Terms) Act 1973 gives exactly the same protection to hire-purchase customers. Section 6(2) (b) of the Unfair Contract Terms Act also prohibits hire-purchase traders and lenders from evading that provision. (See p. 26 for more details about this Act.)

Section 56 of the Consumer Credit Act (see p. 128) provides that the consumer can also sue the credit provider if the supplier misdescribes the goods.

We have explained on p. 17 that tradespersons commit a criminal offence under the Trade Descriptions Act if they attach false descriptions to goods. Businesspersons who deal in hire-purchase goods can also be prosecuted under this Act.

Cancelling the agreement after doorstep talk

Consumers who are talked into buying goods or services which they later realize they do not really want cannot usually do anything about it. In the case of hire-purchase however, the position is different. Customers who are talked into entering hire-purchase agreements on their doorstep are given an opportunity to withdraw from the agreement after a period of reflection. The Consumer Credit Act sets out the circumstances in which customers have the right to cancel the agreement, the length of time they are given to think about it, what customers must do effectively to cancel the agreement and the effect of such cancellation.

Section 67 of the Act sets out which agreements can be cancelled (called 'cancellable agreements'). An HP agreement is cancellable if oral representations are made to the debtor's face (phone calls are not included) by the 'negotiator' (this includes anyone acting on behalf of the seller of goods or the lender of money) and the agreement is signed anywhere *other* than the trade premises of the negotiator, seller or would-be lender. This means that if, for example, someone visits you at home or at work or stops you on the street and then talks you into signing an HP agreement you will have an opportunity to get out of it provided you follow the rules set out below.

Section 68 of the Act sets out how long the consumer is given to reconsider. As will be seen later there are strict rules about what documentation must be sent to consumers before an HP agreement becomes valid. The rules differ according to when the agreement becomes legally binding and whether the agreement is presented personally to the consumer for signing or is sent to him/her for that purpose. If the agreement does not become legally binding on signature then a second copy of it must be sent once it is legally binding. If it does become legally binding on signature then a separate notice reminding consumers of their cancellation rights must be sent within seven days. Either way, if the agreement is 'cancellable' the consumer must receive two separate sets of documentation, the second of which will either consist of a copy of the legally binding agreement containing a statement of cancellation rights or a statement of cancellation rights on its own. The cooling-off period begins on signature and ends five days after receipt of the second set of documentation. Time is counted from the date of receipt by the consumer and not the date of sending by the HP people.

Section 69 of the Act sets out the method by which consumers are to communicate their desire to cancel the agreement. There should be no problem about this because the rules about documentation provide that consumers *must* be sent cancellation forms explaining what to do (see later). However, in case you have lost the form, then the important things to know are that you must notify your desire to cancel *in writing* (just making it clear that you wish to cancel the agreement is sufficient) within the time limit set out above. The written notice must be given or sent to the seller of goods, the lender of the money or the doorstep salesperson. Once you have posted the notice they are deemed to have received it on that date.

Once you have cancelled the agreement the Act provides the following:

1. You can get back all the money you have paid.
2. You are also entitled to the return of any goods handed over in part exchange. If these goods are not returned in substantially the same state within 10 days then you must be given a sum of money equal to the part exchange allowance.
3. You are allowed to keep the HP goods until both the above happen.
4. However, you must keep the HP goods safe and give them back when reimbursed unless the goods are perishable or goods 'which by their nature are consumed by use', e.g. food. The idea of this punitive provision was to deter attempts to pressurize consumers into not exercising their cancellation rights.

Truth in lending: APR

One of the aims of the Consumer Credit Act was to provide that there should be 'truth in lending', i.e. that consumers should be informed of the true costs of borrowing money. As will be seen later, credit quotations, documents that consumers sign before entering HP agreements and most credit advertisements must contain details of the 'APR' (the Annual Percentage Rate) of charge. The quoted APR should express the true cost of the proffered credit. A statement about flat rate interest charges, for example, may sound perfectly straightforward but might in reality be quite misleading.

■ A woman wants to buy something on HP. The cash price is £120 and she is told that the interest charged on this amount will be 10 per cent. Ten per cent of £120 is £12 and the lender demands that the total of £132 be paid off by 12 instalments of £11 each. Now, 10 per cent of £120 may well be £12, but as the borrower will gradually be reducing the amount owed each time she makes a monthly payment, the actual charge for the credit is a lot more than 10 per cent. If the lender was genuinely charging only 10 per cent s/he would be asking for less and less interest each month to take account of the fact that the money owed to him is diminishing each month. But he is not doing so. He is behaving as if the whole £120 was owed for the entire period of 12 months. The rate of interest is therefore in fact much higher than quoted.

The idea of APR therefore is that amongst other things lenders must quote an interest rate that reflects the fact that the main amount of money borrowed is getting smaller all the time. The APR must also reflect the other compulsory costs a consumer may incur as a condition of being lent the money, e.g. legal fees, insurance (but only if the lender insists on the policy being with a particular company) and maintenance contracts (but only if the lender insists on the contract being with a particular person and only if the contract insists on routine visits as opposed to visits only where something goes wrong).

Lenders must work out the APR in the prescribed manner which is currently laid out in the Consumer Credit (Total Charge for Credit) Regulations 1980. The APR is calculated by taking into account:

● How much money is being borrowed.
● The total cost of borrowing it. This is referred to as the 'total charge for credit' and consists of all the interest that is to be charged (on the assumption that the borrower pays it on time) and the compulsory expenses mentioned above.
● The length of time within which the money is to be repaid.

The government have published Consumer Credit Tables to make the calculation easier and if the figures do not fit into the tables there is a formula which must be used instead. You may find these tables in your local library and the Office of Fair Trading gives an explanation of the formula in their publication *Credit Charges*.

In the example quoted above, using the Consumer Credit Tables to calculate the true rate of interest, we come up with the revised figure of 19.5 per cent, a considerable advance on 10 per cent. (See also the court case quoted on p. 160 which also illustrates the difference.)

As all would be lenders have to calculate the APR according to the same principles, it follows that consumers can shop around for credit by comparing the different APRs on offer.

Advertisements

The contents of advertisements for HP or other forms of credit are now strictly controlled by the Consumer Credit Act. Under Section 44 of this Act the government was empowered to issue regulations covering the form and content of such advertisements and the Act states that the regulations are to contain provisions 'with a view to ensuring that, having regard to its subject matter and the amount of detail included in it, an advertisement conveys a fair and reasonably comprehensive indication of the nature of the credit or hire facilities offered by the advertiser and of their true cost to the person using them'.

The Consumer Credit (Advertisement) Regulation 1980 provide different rules for different categories of advertisement. The advertisements are categorized according to how much information the advertiser wishes to give. 'Simple' advertisements, for example, contain no more than a statement of the advertiser's name and business, e.g. 'Bloggs. Money Lenders.' Advertisements with more information are referred to as 'intermediate' or 'full' advertisements, depending on the degree of information included. There is not room here to deal with all the complicated rules but note that all categories of advertisements must present the required or permitted information clearly: excessively small print is not permissible. All full and some intermediate advertisements must contain information about the APR and this statement must be given greater or the same prominence as other statements about credit terms and repayment periods. All intermediate advertisements must contain an address or telephone number to which requests for credit quotations can be directed.

It is a criminal offence to disobey the regulations and the Act provides that other sorts of bad practice in relation to advertisements can lead to prosecution also.

- It is a criminal offence to advertise goods and services for sale on credit terms only. The customer must also be given the option to buy for cash (Section 45).
- It is a criminal offence to put out an advertisement for credit which conveys 'information which in a material respect is false or misleading'. In this connection the Act states: 'Information stating or implying an intention on the advertiser's part which he has not got is false.' The advertiser has the same defences available as if prosecuted under the Trade Description Act (see p. 18) (Section 46).

● It is a criminal offence to send to a minor, with a view to financial gain, any document inviting him/her to borrow money, obtain goods on credit or hire, obtain services on credit or apply for information or advice about borrowing money or otherwise obtaining credit or hiring goods. Would-be lenders can get off by proving that they did not know and had no reason to suspect that the person circularized was a minor, but if they send the document to a school, for example, it will be assumed that they did have grounds for such suspicion (Section 50).

More information about rules governing the advertisements of goods has been given on p. 20.

Quotations

If you look in a shop window you may well see a notice saying something like, 'Instant Credit. Details inside.' The contents of the 'details', or credit quotations as they are called, are now controlled by the Consumer Credit Act. The Consumer Credit (Quotations) Regulations 1980 stipulate that a would-be lender must give a written quotation when asked to do so orally at his trade premises, or when receiving a written request for one or on being telephoned in response to advertisements. The quotation must contain certain information including: the APR (displayed no less prominently than other statements about credit terms and period payments), the name and address of the quoter, the amount of proffered credit, details of any security that will be requested such as a guarantee, cash price of goods, charges additional to those represented in the APR, other liabilities that may arise, the total amount that will have to be paid, the frequency and number of repayments, the amount of each repayment and any different treatment meted out to cash customers. Breach of these requirements is a criminal offence.

Agreeing the deal: the documentation

The Consumer Credit Act strictly controls the form which an HP agreement must take. This contrasts with cash transactions to purchase goods, the formalities for which or the lack of them are entirely a matter of choice for the customer and seller. The Act provides that in relation to HP a number of provisions must be complied with; if they are not lenders can only enforce the agreement by an order of the court which they might not get. (Snatching the goods back would amount to enforcement in this context.) As will be seen later other credit agreements are controlled in the same way. The rules about documentation are contained in Part V of the Act and in the Consumer Credit (Agreements) Regulations 1983 and the Consumer Credit (Cancellation Notices and Copies of Documents) Regulations 1983.

Section 60 deals with the contents of the agreement, which must be such that consumers are made aware of the rights and duties imposed on them by the agreement and the protection and remedies available under the Act. The Regulations provide the agreement must include the following:

- A prominent heading saying: 'Hire Purchase Agreement regulated by the Consumer Credit Act 1974.'
- Name and postal address of the lender and borrower.
- Details of the goods being supplied and their cash price.
- Details of any advance payment.
- Amount of the credit.
- The total charge for the credit.
- The APR displayed prominently as with advertisements and quotations.
- The total amount payable.
- The timing and amount of repayments.
- Details of any security provided by the customer.
- Details of the consumer's rights in relation to cancellation (where applicable), termination, the right to a rebate for early settlement, the right not to have the goods repossessed without a court order and rights in relation to the quality of the goods supplied.

Section 61 goes on to deal with signatures. The agreement must be readily legible, must contain all the compulsory terms (as above) and all other terms except for those implied automatically, e.g. the provisions of the Sale of Goods Act concerning merchantability (see p. 29 and below) and must be signed correctly. This means that once the agreement contains all the necessary ingredients the customer is to sign in a specially designed signature box and the trader is to sign outside the box. If all this is not done the agreement is not 'properly executed' and lenders may not enforce it without a court order which they may not get.

Sections 62, 63 and 64 lay down strict rules about the provision to the customer of copies of the agreement and documents to which it refers, and about the sending of notices informing customers of their rights of cancellation where these apply. Sometimes the agreements does not take legal effect immediately the customer signs it. This is often because the lender has not yet signed. In such a case the agreement is called 'unexecuted'; when it does come into effect it is referred to as being 'executed'. The rules about copies are set out below and note that when we say borrowers must be given a copy of the agreement they must also at the same time be given a notice specifying their rights to cancel where appropriate (see above) and also copies of documents referred to in the agreement.

- If the agreement is presented to the borrower to sign and it remains unexecuted, i.e. it does not come into effect there and then, the borrower must there and then be given a copy of the unexecuted agreement, etc. When and if the agreement later comes into force the borrower must be posted a copy of the now executed agreement, etc., within seven days of the execution.
- If the agreement is presented to the borrower to sign and it does come into effect immediately then seven days later the borrowers must be sent a separate notice telling him/her of his/her rights to cancel. At the time of signing the borrower must also be given a copy of the executed agreement.
- If the agreement is sent to the borrower to sign a copy of it must be sent at the same time. If the agreement comes into force as soon as it is signed by the borrower then no more copies of it will be sent, but s/he will get within seven days a separate notice telling him/her of his/her rights to cancel. If the agreement does not come into force when the borrower signs then within seven days of it taking legal effect the borrower must be sent a copy of the agreement, etc. as executed.

If these rules are not complied with the agreement is regarded as being not 'properly executed' and cannot be enforced without a court order which the lender might not get (see below).

If you later lose the copy agreement that was sent or given to you, Section 77 of the Act gives you the right to write to the lender requesting a copy of the executed agreement *and* a signed statement showing how much has been paid so far, how much is currently owing and how much will be owing in the future. A small fee (50p at present) must be paid. Creditors are bound by whatever answer they give and must reply within 12 working days. If they do not then once one month has gone by they can be prosecuted in the criminal courts and they cannot meanwhile enforce the agreement.

If the agreement was not 'properly executed' then the lender cannot force the borrower to keep to his/her side of the 'bargain' without a court order. Section 127 of the Act provides that the court may not in any circumstances make an order enforcing an agreement if certain rules have been violated.

- The agreement is useless if the consumer has not signed a document containing all the prescribed terms stated above. (It follows that failure to sign in the *directed* way in the box, etc. is not completely fatal.)
- The agreement is useless if the required notices of cancellation were not served.
- The court will not make an order if the lender did not give the consumer the requisite copies of the agreement *and* has not provided a copy of the executed agreement before beginning the court proceedings. It follows that all the lender need do here is hand over a copy and begin again.

In other cases the court should not order that the agreement be enforced unless it considers it 'just to do so'. Considerations taken into account include the degree of prejudice caused to the borrower by the contravention and the degree of culpability by the lender. The court can also instead reduce the sum owed by the borrower, impose conditions, suspend the operation of any order or vary the agreement or any security given under it.

Wishing you hadn't agreed the deal

We have already explained that consumers who are talked into signing an HP agreement on the doorstep are given an opportunity to cancel the agreement (see p. 129). There are other chances to get out of the deal if you later regret entering into it.

As mentioned above, the agreement may not come into force as soon as the consumer signs it because, for example, the lender may not yet have signed. The consumer has a legal right to withdraw from the agreement at any time before it becomes legally binding, so if you have signed it but the lender has not you still have time to get out of it. This right is a common law right (see explanation of principles of contract on p. 5). The Consumer Credit Act, however, regulates the mechanism of your withdrawal. Section 57 of the Act states that a consumer who is still entitled to withdraw from the agreement can effect that withdrawal by communicating with either the seller of the goods, the lender of the money or the negotiator and telling them either verbally or in writing of the withdrawal. Although verbal communication is allowed you obviously should put something in writing so you can prove you did withdraw. The effect of withdrawal from the agreement is the same as cancellation, (see p. 131).

If it is too late to withdraw but you still want to get out of the agreement then you have two further options. Which one you select will depend on whether or not you want to keep the goods and how much money you have available.

Section 94 of the Act gives consumers the right to complete payments ahead of time. In other words, you can if you wish pay off all you owe early. If you do this you will be given a rebate to take accout of this early repayment and you can keep the goods. The amount of the rebate has to be calculated in accordance with the rules set out in the Consumer Credit (Rebate on Early Settlement) Regulations 1983. If you are thinking of doing this and want to know how much you would have to pay then Section 97 gives consumers the right to request in writing details of what it would cost to settle up and the figure quoted must give credit for any rebate to which the consumer would be entitled. The information must be given within 12 working days and a lender who disobeys this can be prosecuted after one month's delay and cannot enforce the agreement meanwhile.

Section 99 of the Act offers another option to HP customers. Such consumers can terminate the agreement at any time but the goods must be returned (unless they can afford to buy them outright) and if the HP company has not received in total to date an amount of money equal to half the purchase price of the goods then it must be given a sum of money to make the payments up to that amount. A court can order a consumer to pay less if that would adequately compensate the lender and can order a consumer to pay extra if the goods have been damaged.

If you want to get out of an HP deal therefore you will have to decide which is the best method for you and which you can afford. If you cannot afford any of these options and you cannot afford the payments either, see p. 143 for the likely consequences.

Guarantees

Sometimes HP companies insist that a consumer find a guarantor before they are prepared to provide the desired credit. A guarantor is someone who agrees with the creditor that s/he will pay up if the borrower fails to do so. The Consumer Credit Act provides some protection to persons who stand as guarantors in respect of HP and other credit agreements.

As with the actual agreement itself there are strict rules about what form a guarantee must take and if these rules are not adhered to the lender cannot enforce the guarantee without a court order which they might not get. See p. 137 for the criteria the court adopts and note that if the main HP agreement cannot for any reason be enforced without a court order then neither can the guarantee unless and until the court makes such an order.

Section 105 of the Act and the Consumer Credit (Guarantees and Indemnities) Regulations 1983 state what must be in a guarantee and the provisions are very similar to those that relate to the main agreement. For example:

- The guarantee must be 'expressed in writing'.
- The guarantee must be 'properly executed'. It must therefore be signed by or on behalf of the surety and must contain all the information which is required by the Regulations. The latter includes telling guarantors what rights they have. The guarantee must be 'readily legible'.
- The guarantor must be given a copy of his/her own agreement and of the agreement which the debtor has signed. Section 107 gives the guarantor the right to demand in writing and on payment of a fee a statement of how much the debtor has paid so far, what is owed at the moment and how much more there is to be paid in the future. The same time limits and sanctions for non-compliance with the request apply as when the debtor requests information (see above, p. 137).

If debtors fail to pay then, as will be seen later, a 'default notice' must be served on them before certain types of action can be taken against them. A copy of this notice must also be served on the guarantor. Once this has been done and the period of paying up has elapsed the guarantor can be asked to pay.

Shoddy and dangerous goods

Consumers who buy goods on hire-purchase or by conditional sale have the same rights as cash customers to be provided with goods that are of merchantable quality and fit for their required purpose. Section 14 of the Sale of Goods Act offers this protection to cash customers (see pp. 29–33) and conditional sale buyers, and HP buyers are given exactly the same rights under Section 10 of the Supply of Goods (Implied Terms) Act 1973. Section 6(2)(b) of the Unfair Contract Terms Act prohibits hirers from evading the provisions by means of an exclusion clause. (See p. 26 for discussion of exclusion clauses.)

■ A company bought a car on HP in October 1979. By January 1980 serious defects had come to light; by the end of March there were 12 further faults and the original defects had not been put right. In June 1980 the exasperated purchasers wrote to the HP company to say they no longer wanted the car. In September 1980 the purchasers demanded their money back or a new car. When neither materialized the buyers sued the HP company for breach of the implied term that the car should be of merchantable quality. The court agreed that the term had been breached and the HP company had to pay up. (Laurelgates v Lombard North Central (1983) 133 NLJ 720)

As far as dangerous goods are concerned, see p. 34 for rights to sue for negligence.

No deal

If someone refuses to sign an HP deal with you, it may be because you appear in the files of a 'credit reference agency'. Most HP companies check up on would-be borrowers before agreeing a deal. If you have ever defaulted on such an agreement or any similar deal before, they can find out about it by consulting one of these agencies. However, an agency might have information on their files about you which is untrue. The Consumer Credit Act now controls this situation and you can put the record straight as follows.

Section 157 of the Act gives consumers the right to know if an HP company or anyone else involved in the abortive deal has consulted a credit reference agency about their financial standing during the 'antecedent negotiations'. The request must be in writing and the lender must receive it within 28 days after the negotiations have ended. The lenders must then within seven working days send to the consumer the name and address of any agency they have consulted and failure to do so is a criminal offence.

Armed with this information the consumer can then demand a copy of the file the agency consulted has on him/her. The request must be in writing, and you must send a fee (presently £1). The agency must then within seven working days send a copy of the file or tell the consumer they do not have one and failure to do so is a criminal offence. A file means all the information the agency has regarding the individual regardless of how that information is stored and obscure abbreviations etc. must be translated into 'plain English'.

If you do not like what you read when you get it you can demand to have it changed, but only if the information is incorrect and if uncorrected likely to prejudice you. In such an event you may write to the agency 'requiring it either to remove the entry from the file or amend it'. The agency must then within 28 days write to the consumer to say whether or not they are going to remove or amend the offending entry. If the answer is 'yes,' the agency must also within 10 days give notice of the amendment to all those to whom they gave information about the consumer's financial standing during the previous six months. They must also give the consumer a copy of the amendment.

If you are not satisfied with the reply you get or if you hear nothing at all, you may still persist with your complaint. Within 28 days of hearing from the agency (or after 28 days if they do not write) you may send to them a notice of correction, (maximum length 200 words) containing the text of the required amendment and demanding that this be added to the file. Faced with this missive the agency has a choice. Within 28 days they must either notify the consumer that they will comply with the notice (in which case they must tell the same people as above) or they must apply to the Director General of Fair Trading for permission to refuse to do so.

If you are not satisfied with that either then within 28 days (or after 28 days if you hear nothing) you too may apply to the Director General, asking for the entry to be deleted or altered. You must state in your letter the name and address of the agency, when the notice of correction was sent, particulars of the objectionable entry, why it is incorrect and why failure to correct it will be prejudicial to you. The Director will make such order as s/he thinks fit and the agency commits a criminal offence if they do not obey. If they are ordered to amend an entry they must also notify the same people as above.

If you feel that simple amendment is not enough to compensate you, you may consider reporting the offending agency to your local trading standards officer. Persons operating credit reference agencies must be licensed and keeping bogus information might lead to the offender's licence being revoked. Also you might be able to sue for damages under e.g. the Data Protection Act 1984 but take advice about this first.

Discrimination

In order to do HP business lawfully the lender must have a licence and these are only supposed to be granted to 'fit persons'. Section 25 of the Consumer Credit Act states that one criterion to be taken into account is whether the applicant has 'practised discrimination on grounds of sex, colour, race or ethnic origins in, or in connection with, the carrying on of any business'. It follows that a person granted a licence might well later lose it if the Director General was satisfied that s/he had been indulging in discriminatory practices.

Additionally, the Sex Discrimination Act 1975 and Race Relations Act 1976 both provide that it is unlawful for a person concerned in the provision of facilities or services to discriminate against a customer on grounds of race or sex. (These Acts do not apply in Northern Ireland but there is an Order making similar provision in respect of sex discrimination.) Facilities or services include 'facilities by way of banking or insurance or for grants, loans, credit or finance'. It is therefore unlawful to refuse credit on the basis of race or sex or to refuse to provide credit in the like matter and on the like terms 'as are normal in relation to other customers'.

■ An employed married woman agreed to buy a suite of furniture at a retail store. She paid two deposits and asked to pay the rest by HP, but was told she would not be given HP facilities unless her husband agreed to stand as her guarantor. She understandably enquired whether she would have been asked to stand as guarantor for her husband if he were to request HP facilities and was answered in the negative. Her husband then signed the guarantee form and the suite was later delivered to her. The store admitted in writing that they would not have imposed a guarantor requirement on a married man whose circumstances were in all material respects similar to hers. The court held that the store's behaviour amounted to unlawful discrimination. (Quinn v Williams Furniture Ltd (1981) 1CR 328 CA)

Can't pay, won't pay

Can't pay

What can the HP company do to you if you fall behind with your payments? This situation too is now controlled by the provisions of the Consumer Credit Act.

If an HP company wants to end the agreement, recover the HP goods or make your guarantor pay up then they must first serve you with what is called a 'default notice'. This is stated in Section 87 of the Consumer Credit Act, and the Consumer Credit (Enforcement, Default and Termination Notices) Regulations 1983 set out the compulsory format and contents of the notice. Amongst other things the notice must specify what breach of the agreement the consumer is guilty of, the action necessary to put matters right, and what the HP company intends to do if you do not comply. The consumer is to be given at least seven days in which to pay up and if the consumer does what is asked the breach is treated as never having taken place.

Section 90 of the Consumer Credit Act also protects the consumer against having HP goods seized by the HP company. If the consumer gets behind with payments the HP company cannot seize the goods without a court order if the consumer has already paid one third of the total price. If the HP company disobeys this rule then the consumer can get back by court action all the money paid by him/her under the agreement. Section 92 also provides that HP companies are not permitted under any circumstances to enter the consumer's home to recover goods without a court order. If they do so the consumer can sue them for damages.

A consumer who receives a default notice can apply to the court for a 'time order', which will enable you to pay off the arrears by instalments. Note too that the HP company cannot charge a higher rate of interest on the arrears than the rate you were paying already. If you do not get round to applying to the court but the HP company do so later you can still ask for a time order then. The court can additionally make an order that is suspended, i.e. will not come into force as long as you do something such as pay instalments. The court is also allowed to make an order permitting you to keep some of the goods but ordering you to return the rest to the HP company.

Won't pay

If, despite all the safeguards which are supposed to protect you from entering into an unwise credit situation, you still succeed in landing yourself with an extortionate agreement then it may be possible to apply to the court to vary what has been agreed. The Consumer Credit Act provides that a court may reopen any credit bargain (i.e. no price limits) which it finds to be extortionate. Section 138 of the Act sets out a number of criteria to which the court is to have regard in determining if the agreement is extortionate. The court should look at other interest rates prevailing at the time and the age, experience, business capacity and state of health of the borrower and the degree to which s/he was under financial pressure at the time of entering into the agreement. The court can also consider factors like the degree of risk the lender took on. If the court is satisfied the agreement is extortionate it can amongst other things alter the terms (see example on page 160).

10.

Borrowing money to buy goods or services

Here we deal with consumers' rights when using forms of credit other than HP or conditional sale to pay for goods or services in situations where the provider of credit is either the same person as is selling the goods or services or is linked with them in some way. These include:

- purchases of goods and services by credit card;
- purchases made in shops by use of an account sometimes called a 'budget account'; and
- the purchase of goods by credit sale agreement. This is an agreement where the consumer becomes the legal owner of the goods at the outset but pays for the goods by instalments. (It is different from HP because in an HP agreement the goods do not become the consumer's property until all the instalments have been paid.)

These sorts of agreement are also in the main controlled by the provisions of the Consumer Credit Act, but the Act does not cover the following situations:

- If the total amount of credit on offer exceeds £15,000 (£5,000 if the agreement was made before 20 May 1985) the Act does not apply. The rules are complicated so if in doubt whether your transaction is protected, take advice.
- If you have a card, shop or other trading account and the agreement is that you must pay off the total owing at the end of a particular period then the act does not apply. This means, for example, that American Express and Diners Club cards are not covered but cards like Access and Barclaycard are.
- If the money advanced has to be paid off by not more than four instalments the agreement is not covered. This provision

takes most accounts like milk bills and grocery bills out of the Act's control and could exempt a credit sale agreement.

If the agreement is what the Act calls a 'small agreement' then some but not all of the provisions of the Act will apply. A small agreement is one where the credit does not exceed £50. Thus credit cards and accounts will not be covered if the total credit on offer does not exceed £50, and credit sales would not be covered if the purchase price minus deposit and charges paid by the customer did not exceed £50. We will point out as we go along which protection is not available to small agreements.

As with HP, persons providing credit in situations where the Act does apply must be licensed by the Director General of Fair Trading, and they commit a criminal offence if they carry on such business without a licence. Agreements made by unlicensed persons can only be enforced against the borrower with the permission of the Director General and this is likely to be given only in extenuating circumstances.

Sales talk

Misrepresentation, misdescription and trade description

Consumers paying by credit card, store account or credit sale have the same rights to sue sellers or service persons for misrepresentation or misdescription as purchasers paying by any other means. The Consumer Credit Act gives the consumer the added advantage of being able to sue not only the seller or service person but also the provider of credit. These rights derive partly from the provisions of Section 56 of the Act (see p. 128 in relation to hire-purchase) whereby representations made by a supplier are deemed to be made by the lender as well if the two have some business connection with each other. In addition, Section 75 of the Consumer Credit Act provides that where such a connection exists customers have the same rights against the lender in respect of misrepresentations or breaches of contract as they already have against the supplier. This has other implications, e.g. in relation to shoddy goods and services, as we shall see later. *But* Section 75 only applies if the goods bought cost more than £100 or less that £30,000. There is no such price limitation in respect of Section 56.

The result is that if suppliers make untrue or inaccurate statements about goods or services paid for by credit cards the consumer may be able to sue both the supplier *and* the credit card company by virtue of either or both of these sections of the Consumer Credit Act.

As already explained, sellers of goods and services can be prosecuted under the Trade Descriptions Act if they make untrue statements about what they are selling, and the same applies if the consumer pays for the items by means of credit card, store account or credit sale.

Sales print

APR

In the previous chapter (p. 131) we explained what is meant by the expression 'APR.' Any quoted APR should express the true cost of the desired credit and, as all lenders must use the same method to calculate it, consumers should be able to shop around for the best deal. How does this system work in respect of the agreements we are now discussing?

With credit sale, the rules are the same as for HP agreements (see p. 131).

Credit cards and store account agreements, where the same interest rate is charged at regular intervals, usually monthly, are called 'running account' credit by the Consumer Credit Act. (Credit agreements like HP where it is known at the outset exactly how much the consumer is to borrow are called 'fixed sum' agreements.) With a credit card account, for example, it is not known how much will actually be borrowed within the permitted credit limit.

As with the APR of fixed sum credit agreements, the APR of running account credit agreements must similarly reflect any compulsory costs the borrower will be put to, the rate of interest that will be charged in relation to any money borrowed and in addition the frequency with which interest charges will be made. The APR will not however reflect how often within the charging period the interest calculation is made. You might, for instance, see statements like 'interest of 2% of the balance outstanding will be charged to your account at the end of the month', or: 'Interest will be charged on a daily basis at the rate of 2% per month.' In the first case 2 per cent is charged on whatever sum the consumer owes at the end of the month. In the second example the amount of 2 per cent interest charged is based on the contents of the account each day although the actual charge itself is only levied monthly. Depending on how the account is operated by the borrower this could make a considerable difference to the amount paid for the credit. However, the expressed APR of both example agreements would be the same, i.e. 26.8 per cent. The same regulations do provide, however, that borrowers must be told not just what the APR is but also how frequently the interest calculation will be made.

Advertisements, quotations and unsolicited credit tokens

The rules relating to advertisements and quotations are the same as for HP so see p. 133.

At one time large numbers of credit cards were mailed to unwilling consumers which caused considerable annoyance. Section 51 of the Consumer Credit Act now provides that it is a criminal offence to 'give a person a credit token if he has not asked for it'. 'Give' includes delivering or posting the unwanted item. The term 'credit token' includes credit cards but not cheque cards, and could include bank cash till cards if these offer a credit facility. If the customer has asked for the card to be sent then no offence is committed but the request must be signed by him/her. It also is not an offence to send a replacement credit card without being asked, but a copy of the agreement you signed originally must be sent with it (unless the credit offered is no more than £50).

Agreeing the deal

The documentation of these agreements is controlled in the same way as HP agreements are, with the exception of small agreements which are not subject to any of these provisions.

The rules in Sections 60, 61, 62 and 63 of the Consumer Credit Act all apply, which means that these agreements must be in the correct format and signed in the correct way otherwise they will be considered as being not 'properly executed' with the same sanctions resulting against the lender as apply to not properly executed HP agreements. Customers must also be given copies of the agreement and notices of cancellation rights where appropriate. However, with credit cards there is one change in the rules. The obligation to send a copy of the executed agreement seven days after it came into force is modified to state that it is sufficient for customers to get their copy of the agreement before or at the same time as they receive their card.

The same regulations set out what the agreement must contain. The heading must state clearly that the agreement is controlled by the Act if that is the case. Borrowers must be informed about interest rates, etc. and of their rights including their position if their card is stolen (see later).

Section 78 of the Act provides that in relation to credit card deals and store accounts the borrower may write and demand a copy of the agreement and details of the state of the account, i.e. any amount presently owing and what will be owed and when on the assumption the borrower doesn't borrow any more. A small fee (presently 50p) has to be paid. Credit sales customers have the same rights in this respect under Section 77 as with HP (see p. 136). Section 78 also stipulates that in the case of running account credit, information must automatically be provided to the customer. The information must be sent for each period for which interest is charged unless there has been no movement on the account and anyway at least once a year. The borrower must be told the balance at the beginning and end of the period, details of payments in and out (sufficiently identified) and the amount of any interest and other charges (with enough information so that the borrower knows the basis on which this has been calculated). In all cases the lender must send the information within 12 working days and if they do not do so after a month they can be prosecuted and cannot meanwhile enforce the agreement.

Getting out of the deal

A consumer who has been talked into signing an HP agreement outside trade premises has the right under the Consumer Credit Act to get out of it after a period of reflection. The same rules apply (with two differences set out below) to the sorts of credit agreements dealt with in this chapter which come within the ambit of the Act.

- If the agreement is a small agreement there is no right to cancel under these provisions.
- In the case of credit cards, as with HP, the credit card company must send the consumer a separate notice of cancellation rights in those cases where the agreement comes into immediate effect as soon as the consumer signs it. However, there is no seven-day time limit within which this must be done. As long as the consumer gets the notice before

or at the same time as s/he receives the credit card that is sufficient.

The right to withdraw from the agreement before it comes into force applies equally to the agreements we are discussing here as it does to HP, so see p. 137. Note too that the provisions of Section 57 of the Act which set out the mechanism by which consumers can communicate their withdrawal also apply to the agreements under this heading with the exception of small agreements.

The right to put an end to the agreement by paying everything of ahead of time also applies to agreements under this section. The provisions of Section 94 and 97 under which consumers can pay off early and thereby obtain a rebate and can also demand advance information about what they will have to pay are explained on p. 138.

Guarantees

The position is the same as for hire-purchase (see p. 139), but note that in respect of credit card and store accounts the guarantor has the right under Section 108 of the Act to the same sort of information as the borrower can demand (see above).

Lost or stolen credit cards

What if your card is sent to you but never arrives or is lost or stolen and later misused by somebody else? Who loses out, you or the credit company? The answer, you will be pleased to hear, is usually the credit company but you may be liable if you gave the card to the person who misused it.

Except when you never received the card in the first place, (see below) you can forfeit a *maximum* of £50. This can be avoided if you notify the credit company orally (telephoning is included) before the card is misused, but if your credit agreement demands (and it inevitably will) that you must confirm what you said in writing within 7 days then you *must* do so to avoid losing the £50. The credit company must provide you with a name, address and telephone number for the purpose and if they fail to do so they cannot even claim the £50. These provisions are set out in Sections 83 and 84 of the Consumer Credit Act.

You are not liable for any misuse of a card unless you (or anyone else who under the agreement is allowed to use it) have signed it or a receipt for it or have used it. This is stated in Section 66 of the Act and it follows from that that if the card was stolen before you even received it you cannot be made to forfeit anything.

Shoddy and dangerous goods and services

A customer who pays for goods or services by credit card, store account or credit sale has the same rights as do cash buyers to sue the seller or service person for breach of the Sale of Goods Act, the Supply of Goods and Services Act, or for other breaches of contract or for negligence (see Part I).

Under the provisions of Section 75 and Section 56 of the Consumer Credit Act (see above pp. 128 and 146) these types of credit buyer can also sue the provider of credit where that person has a business connection with the seller. The credit supplier is liable for the seller's or service person's breaches of contract, including breach of statutory provisions. But the goods must have cost *not less* than £100 and not more than £30,000 for the lender to be liable for any such breaches. Be warned too that some credit card companies are trying to evade responsibility in this area in respect of credit cards issued before 1 July 1977. If this happens to you take advice, as they should not be able to get away with it.

No deal

You have the same rights in relation to credit reference agencies and discrimination as when buying goods on HP (see p. 140).

Can't pay, won't pay

Can't pay

What if you fall behind with your instalments when tied up in a credit card, store account or credit sale agreement? As with hire-purchase transactions, Section 87 of the Consumer Credit Act stipulates that a default notice must be served on the debtor before the lender can take certain sorts of punitive action such as ending the agreement, demanding earlier repayment of the debt or making a guarantor pay up. The contents of the default notice must be the same as with hire-purchase, so see p. 143. However, a credit card company does not have to serve a default notice before they 'restrict or defer' your right to credit. They can tell shops and banks not to honour your credit card without being legally obliged to warn you first. You can also be sued for any arrears owing on the agreement without first getting a default notice.

Debtors under credit card, credit sale and store account agreements are also entitled to apply to the court for a time order when they receive a default notice and cannot be charged a higher rate of interest on arrears).

Won't pay

The rules about extortionate credit bargains are as set out above, see p. 144.

11.

Borrowing money

In the previous chapter we set out what rights a consumer has when buying goods or services on credit from a supplier who has some sort of connection with the person lending the money. Such agreements are referred to as 'debtor–creditor–supplier' agreements in the Consumer Credit Act. Agreements where there is no connection between the lender and the supplier are referred to as 'debtor–creditor' agreements, and in some areas the rights of a consumer differ depending on which of the two categories their credit agreement falls into. In this chapter we deal with three forms of credit which normally fall into the debtor–creditor category, namely personal loans (i.e. loans of money from, for example, a finance house), pawnbroking transactions and bank overdrafts.

These agreements are now in the main also controlled by the Consumer Credit Act and those who carry out this sort of business must be licensed. Apart from the provisions regarding extortionate credit which apply without limit, agreements where the total amount of credit exceeds £15,000 (£5,000 if the agreement was made before 20 May 1985) are not covered by the Act. Nor are transactions with a low rate of interest, i.e. where the APR does not exceed 13 per cent or 1 per cent above base bank lending rate, whichever is the higher. The rules about these provisions are complicated so take advice if you are not sure if your agreement is covered. It is a criminal offence to carry out the business of money-lending or pawnbroking without a licence.

■ A man named Mr Curr ran a mobile greengrocery and drapery business and, as a side-line, lent money to customers at high rates of interest (800 per cent, it was later calculated). Sometimes he gave the customer a repayment card and received weekly repayments. Sometimes he took the customer's child benefit or pension book as security and insisted the customer sign the books up in advance and authorize him to collect the money. He was charged with the criminal offence of carrying on a consumer credit business without a licence. He pleaded guilty and was sent to prison and fined. (Regina v Curr 1982 CCLR 13)

Bank overdrafts are exempted from some to the provisions of the Act, e.g. the documentation requirements. However, bank overdrafts are covered by other provisions of the Act whereas the operation of a current account whilst it remains in credit are not.

Misrepresentation, misdescription and trade description

If you happen to use money borrowed to purchase goods or services then you have the same rights against the seller or service person in respect of untrue statements made to you before the purchase took place as if you had paid by cash (see Part I). But in the case of the agreements dealt with in this chapter you will not usually be able to sue the lender for the misrepresentations or breaches of contract of the seller or service person. This is because the provisions of Section 56 and Section 75 of the Consumer Credit Act cover only debtor–creditor–supplier agreements. Personal loans, pawns and overdrafts are usually debtor–creditor agreements. If you could establish some connection between such a lender and the offending supplier you might be able to sue the lender as well. You would have to show that either there were pre-existing arrangements between lender and supplier or, in the case of a loan for a fixed amount, that such arrangements were contemplated. This is a difficult area of law and you should take advice. If the lenders themselves said something untrue about the deal you could possibly then sue them for misrepresentation or breach of contract.

With misdescribed goods the position is the same as above. If the seller of goods misdescribes them the consumer can sue that person for breach of Section 13 of the Sale of Goods Act (see p. 16). However, the lender could only be sued if the agreement is in the debtor–creditor–supplier category.

If lies are told about goods or services bought with the borrowed money then the seller or service person who made the untrue statements could be prosecuted under the Trade Description Act. If the lenders themselves said something untrue about the loan deal then they could lay themselves open to prosecution for making an untrue statement about a service, accommodation or facility (see p. 66).

Doorstep talk and canvassing

The Consumer Credit Act now provides that it is a criminal offence to call uninvited at somebody's home and then try to talk him/her into entering a debtor–creditor agreement such as a personal loan.

Section 49 of the Act states: 'It is an offence to canvass debtor–creditor agreements off trade premises'. Section 48 explains what is meant by canvassing. The offence is committed if 'oral representations' are made to an individual somewhere other than his/her or the lender's business premises so as to 'solicit' the entry of a consumer into the making of a debtor–creditor agreement. The lender can only get off if the consumer had previously signed a written request for such a visit to take place. Therefore, if someone calls on you at home without a previous written invitation and tries to talk you into entering into a personal loan you should report him/her to your local trading standards officer.

There is an exception for bank overdrafts. If the consumer already holds a current account no offence is committed if s/he is verbally encouraged to overdraw on it.

■ A licensed money-lender was accused of 11 offences of canvassing. He had called at 11 households after receiving oral requests via the telephone, etc. for loans of money. A judge commented: 'During his visit, when he was asked for money he laid down the terms on which he was prepared to lend it, as it was a matter of business. Those terms were favourable, in some cases very favourable to him. An example of one of the terms was the handing over of the borrower's benefit allowance book as a 'security' for the proposed loan. The money-lender was found guilty of canvassing as he had not received a *written* request to call as required by the Consumer Credit Act. He tried to argue that he was not guilty because what he had done did not amount to 'soliciting'. This argument did not succeed. (Regina v Chaddha (1984) CCLR 1)

Cancelling the agreement after doorstep talk

Personal loans and pawn agreements are cancellable in the same circumstances as are HP agreements, so see p. 129 for details. The same obligations also exist to serve the consumer with a 'notice of cancellation rights' and the same sanction for failure to do so, namely the loss of the right to enforce the agreement also applies. Pawnbrokers, however, can also be prosecuted in the criminal courts if they do not serve such a notice. This is stated in Section 115 of the Consumer Credit Act.

The provisions regarding cancellation do not apply to bank overdrafts.

APR

We have already explained on p. 131 the meaning of the term 'APR' and that its purpose is to inform the consumer of the true cost of obtaining credit. The position with the sorts of agreement we are dealing with here is as follows:

- **Personal loans and pawns**. If a loan is to be repaid by instalments, the APR will be based on the same principles as for HP, so see p. 131. If the loan plus interest and other expenses is to be paid back in one go, the APR is calculated by working out how much each pound lent has cost the borrower and expressing this as an annual rate.
- **Bank overdrafts**. Banks must tell prospective borrowers what their interest rates are in relation to overdrafts. The interest rate must be calculated as if an APR was being quoted, but incidental charges, e.g. charges per cheque, are not reflected in the figure.

Advertisements and quotations

The control of credit advertisements and quotations by the Consumer Credit Act has been detailed on p. 133. The same controls are also exercised over advertisements for personal loans and pawns. Banks must quote their interest rates calculated on the basis explained above, and must also specify what other charges will be made in relation to overdraft facilities.

Agreeing the deal

Personal loans

The documentation of personal loan agreements is controlled in the same way as HP agreements are. The provisions of Section 60, 61, 62 and 63 of the Consumer Credit Act all apply. Thus a personal loan agreement must be in the correct format, and signed in the correct way, otherwise it will be considered as being not 'properly executed' with the same sanctions resulting against the lender as apply to not properly executed HP agreements. People who enter into personal loan agreements must similarly be given copies of the agreement and notices of cancellation rights where appropriate. (See p. 134 for more details of the provisions and sanctions for not obeying them.)

As with HP too the Consumer Credit (Agreements) Regulations 1983 set out what must be put in a personal loan agreement. If the agreement is controlled by the Act, it must have a prominent heading saying 'Credit Agreement regulated by the Consumer Credit Act 1974,' and give the name and address of creditor and debtor, the amount of credit being provided, the total charge for credit, the APR and the timing and amounts of repayments. If a security has been provided then details of this must be included, and details of charges payable if the debtor defaults. Debtors must also be told of their rights to cancel where appropriate and of their rights to settle up ahead of time. Anyone serving as a guarantor for a personal loan has the same rights as if guaranteeing an HP deal (see p. 139).

Consumers who enter personal loan agreements also have the same rights under Section 77 of the Act to write and ask for copies of the agreement and details of how much is owing as do HP customers (see p. 136).

Pawns

If a consumer pawns something to obtain a loan then the lender must adhere to the above requirements regarding documentation. But there is an additional sanction against pawnbrokers. If the provisions of Section 62, Section 63 or Section 64 (duty to provide copies of unexecuted and executed agreement and to serve notices of cancellation where appropriate) are not kept to then the pawnbroker can be prosecuted in the criminal courts.

Additionally Section 114 of the Act states that if an article is taken into pawn then the consumer must at the same time be given a 'pawn receipt,' which must be in the correct format. Failure to do this is also a criminal offence. The receipt can either be included as part of the main agreement, in which case its contents are controlled by the same regulations, or it can form a separate document, in which case its contents are regulated by the Consumer Credit (Pawn Receipts) Regulations 1983. In either case, there must be a description of the pawned article sufficient to identify it, a notice to customers telling them of their rights to redeem, the date by which such rights may be lost, what to do if the receipt is lost, what will happen if the article is not redeemed (see below for more about these issues) and a warning if the pawnbroker does not intend to insure the article whilst in their custody. The pawnbroker must also sign and date the receipt.

Note too that it is a criminal offence for pawnbrokers to take a pawn from someone who they know or who appears to be a minor.

Bank overdrafts.

These are exempt from the rules about documentation set out in Sections 60, 61, 62, 63, 64 of the Consumer Credit Act, but Section 78 does apply. Thus information about the state of the account can be demanded and must be given (see p. 149).

Getting out of the deal

A consumer who has entered into a personal loan agreement can withdraw at any time before the agreement comes into force. As with HP, Section 57 of the Consumer Credit Act regulates the method of communication of withdrawal. A personal loan can also be paid off early and a rebate obtained.

A consumer who has pawned something may well wish to pay off the loan and retrieve the pawned object. The Consumer Credit Act, Sections 116 and 117, controls your rights in this respect. Whilst the pawn remains 'redeemable' (see below) the pawnbroker must give it back if presented with the pawn receipt and all the money owing. Failure to do so is a criminal offence unless the pawnbroker knows or has reason to suspect that the person who turns up with the pawn receipt has stolen it. If a consumer loses the pawn receipt, Section 118 states that s/he can instead produce a statutory declaration (this is a formal oath sworn in front of a solicitor or JP) or in the case of loans or credit limits below £25 a statement in writing will do.

A pawn must remain 'redeemable' for a minimum of six months but the consumer and pawnbroker can agree that it is to be redeemable for a longer period. If the loan or credit limit was for no more that £25 the pawn can no longer be redeemed after the redemption period. In all other cases the pawn remains 'redeemable' until the pawnbroker sells it, and the consumer must usually be given advance warning of this (see below).

No deal

The rules about credit reference agencies and discrimination are the same for agreements covered in this chapter as for HP (see p. 140).

Can't pay, won't pay

Can't pay

Personal loans
If borrowers who have signed a personal loan agreement controlled by the Consumer Credit Act get behind with their payments then the lender cannot take certain sorts of punitive action without first serving a default notice. This is stated in Section 87 of the Act. The sorts of punitive action forbidden before service of the notice include ending the agreement, demanding earlier repayment of the borrowed money and enforcing a security, e.g. demanding payment from a gurantor. The default notice must contain the same sort of information as in the case of HP agreements and the consumer has the same rights to apply to the court for a time order. (See p. 143 for more details.)

Note that there is no need for a lender to serve a default notice before suing for the arrears alone.

Pawns
What happens if you cannot afford to redeem an article that has been pawned? There comes a time when the pawnbroker is entitled to sell the object but the Consumer Credit Act, Sections 120 and 121, regulates the procedure and provides that the pawnbroker must usually warn the consumer first and give the consumer any excess profits thus made.

The pawnbroker is entitled to sell the pawn once the agreed redemption period or six months (whichever is the longer) has passed. First, though, the pawnbroker must notify the consumer of their intention to sell the object *unless* the loan or credit limit was for less than £50, in which case they do not have to bother. The Consumer Credit (Realization of Pawn) Regulations 1983 specify what this notice must contain and the compulsory information includes details of when and where the object will be offered for sale. Consumers must also be reminded that if they pay what is owed and surrender the pawn receipt without delay the sale will not take place. The notice must give at least 14 days' warning.

Once the sale has taken place the pawnbroker must send the borrower another notice within 20 working days. Once again though, if the loan or credit limit provided was for under £50 they need not bother. The notice must say when the sale took place, what price was got for the pawn, the itemized expenses of selling it, what the figure owed on the loan was on the date of sale and what is consequently owing to borrower or to the lender. If there is any dispute about whether the pawnbroker obtained the true market value of the pawn or charged unreasonably high expenses, the onus to justify both is on the pawnbroker who must also pay any surplus owing to the borrower.

Overdrafts

The position is the same as for credit cards. Banks do not have to give notice under the Consumer Credit Act before suspending or terminating an overdraft facility.

Won't pay

As explained on p. 144, the court can reopen any credit bargain on the grounds that it is extortionate. The example below which relates to a loan from a finance company illustrates this law in action.

■ Mr and Mrs Edwards borrowed £400 from a finance company. They agreed to repay the loan in full by 12 monthly instalments of £66.66. The agreement stated that the interest rate was 84 per cent. Actually it was a great deal more than that. The couple would have paid a total of £799 by the end of the year. The true annual flat rate of interest was nearer 100 per cent therefore, and the APR a staggering 319 per cent.

The unfortunate pair used the £400 to purchase a car that turned out to be such a bad buy that they were later obliged to sell it for scrap for a miserly £30. Later they fell behind with their repayments to the finance company, who sued for their money. The Edwardses in turn argued that the interest charged was exhorbitant, relying on the provisions of Section 138 of the Consumer Credit Act. The judge agreed with them. One factor he took into account was the fact that other finance companies at that time were making similar loans at flat rates of 18–20 per cent. He therefore altered the agreement to 40 per cent flat rate, giving a total owing of £560, as opposed to £799. (Barcabe Ltd v Edwards and Another (1983) CCLR 11)

Part IV
Dealing with Problems

12.

Getting advice and further information

At various points in this book we have advised the reader to 'take advice'. This may have been because the law on the particular issue was too complex to be fully discussed here. Consumers should also, if possible, always seek advice if the loss suffered was large or where personal injury has occurred. You may also feel that an official-looking letter would be more effective than one sent by you.

Two factors often deter people from seeking advice even when they need it. One is not knowing where to go and the other is fearing the cost of such advice. In this chapter we detail which agencies offer free advice and the extent to which they can help you. We also list other agencies who could assist and who do or might charge something. Thirdly we advise about consulting a lawyer and the scope of the legal aid scheme.

Free advice agencies

Citizens advice bureaux

Those who have entered into credit agreements may have noticed in their documentation an invitation to consult their local Citizens Advice Bureau (CAB) if they want to find out more about the protection provided by the Consumer Credit Act. Citizens Advice Bureaux are widely spread around the country. They give advice on a considerable range of matters including consumer problems. Their advice is free and confidential. Many of the staff in these Bureaux are volunteers but all have received training. Very few Bureaux have in-house solicitors but local solicitors often operate free advice sessions in the evenings. Besides advising, the Bureau may be able to:

- send letters on behalf of members of the public on their headed notepaper;
- help a consumer negotiate with a trader or trading association and help a consumer in arbitration with the latter;
- offer advice and help to consumers taking cases to court. (They cannot 'represent' a consumer in court because of the lawyers' monopoly, see p. 81.)

Whether a Citizens Advice Bureau would actually agree to do all or any of the above would depend on how busy they were but they will always refer people to someone who can help where they cannot. Look in the phone book for the address of your nearest CAB.

Consumer Advice Centres

These are funded by local authorities and provide the same sort of service to the public as the CABs except that they specialize in consumer affairs.

Law Centres

In some areas Law Centres have been set up. They have qualified lawyers on their staff and so are able to represent people in court. They do not charge people for their services. They employ advice workers and often also operate free advice sessions in the evenings which local lawyers attend. Whether or not a Law Centre would be able to help with a consumer problem would depend on what types of work the Law Centre in question had decided to take on, but they will refer you to someone else who can help if they cannot.

The local authority

Although your local authority may have chosen not to fund a Consumer Advice Centre they must have a Trading Standards Department so that traders who have broken the criminal law can be brought to book. Apart from being a good place to report traders to, this department may be prepared to give consumers general advice. Ring your county council (or London Borough Council, the Regional and Island Council in Scotland, or the District Council in Northern Ireland) and ask for the Trading Standards Department (or it may be called the Consumer Protection or Consumer Services Department).

Consumer groups

The Consumers Association (*Which?*)

The Consumers association publishes the well-known magazine *Which?* and also offers a consumer advice service, 'Which? Personal Service', to those who pay an annual subscription (currently £20.00). (This does not cover getting the magazine.) The service aims primarily to help consumers to help themselves, e.g. by drafting letters for the consumer to send or by helping consumers to start court proceedings themselves. But *Which?* will also use their considerable influence to intervene directly with retailers, manufacturers or suppliers if they consider this would be the best way of achieving a successful outcome. If *Which?* considers your case raises important matters of principle relevant to the interests of consumers as a whole, they might be prepared to pay legal costs. If you want to join, the address is Which? Personal Services, 14 Buckingham Street, London WC2N 6DS. Tel: 01-839 7521/2

Local consumer groups

Encouraged by the Consumers Association, various local consumer groups have sprung up. If there is one in your area you might be able to get help and advice from them if you have a consumer problem. As such groups receive no public funding they may well ask you to pay a fee to join and whether or not they can give advice about the particular problem would depend on their knowledge and resources. If you want to know if there is such a group near you, you can write to the National Federation of Consumer Groups, 12 Mosley Street, Newcastle-upon-Tyne NE1 1DE. Tel: 0632 618259. If there is no local group for you to join, you can join the federation direct as an individual or they will advise you how to start a group yourself!

Consulting a lawyer

Before consulting a lawyer the consumer will first have to see a solicitor. (See section on lawyers on p. 81.) Solicitors who are in 'private practice', i.e. not employed in a Law Centre or other institution, obviously charge for their services but sometimes their fees are paid for by the state via a means-tested legal aid scheme. Below we explain how this scheme operates and also give advice about choosing solicitors and how to deal with them. When is it worth consulting a solicitor? It is certainly worth it for those who have suffered serious injury or substantial economic loss. This is because legal proceedings will probably have to be taken, or at the very least threatened, and because the calculation of what damages are properly owed is a complicated business in serious cases and beyond the scope of most of the agencies mentioned above. If the claim is not a substantial one, consulting a lawyer may not be very cost-effective particularly as the amount of legal costs you could recover in a small claims case in the County Court is severely restricted (see later, p. 203). If in doubt about whether to go to a solicitor or not you could always seek advice from one of the other agencies first.

Legal aid

There are various different types of legal aid as follows:

- The 'green form' scheme ('pink form' in Scotland). Under this scheme a solicitor may offer advice, write letters, make telephone calls, negotiate on a client's behalf and obtain a barrister's opinion. It is the solicitor who means-tests the client. Those whose income is too high are excluded from the scheme altogether. Those whose income is very low, e.g. those on supplementary benefit, have nothing to pay, and those in between have to make a one-off contribution towards the lawyer's fees. The lawyer must ask permission from the legal aid authorities before being allowed to do more than £50 worth of work. The lawyer is not entitled to do anything at all unless a question of law is involved, but this would cover most consumer problems, e.g. breach of contract, misrepresentation and negligence.
- The 'fixed fee' interview scheme. This scheme is suitable for those excluded from the green form scheme and those who would have to make a large contribution under it. Under this scheme the solicitor will charge a maximum of £5 inclusive of VAT for up to half an hour of advice.
- Legal aid to take court proceedings. Neither of the above schemes covers actually suing someone in court. For this a separate legal aid application must be made. The solicitor will complete the form and ask the consumer to sign it. This form will contain information about the consumer's financial situation and will set out the basis of the consumer's claim.

Whether or not legal aid will be granted depends on two factors. First, the merits of the case must be considered. Legal aid can be refused if the consumer does not have 'reasonable grounds' for taking the proceedings, i.e. there is no reasonable prospect of them winning. It can also be refused if any advantage gained would be trivial. This latter could present a problem where small consumer claims are involved but those where, for example, serious personal injury has resulted would obviously not be disqualified under this head. If legal aid is refused on the merits of the case the consumer can appeal. The second factor is the consumer's finances. These will be assessed by the DHSS. Some people will not qualify at all, others will get the court representation for nothing and others will have to contribute towards it by a lump sum or by instalments.

More information about legal aid can be obtained from:

- The Law Society, The Law Society's Hall, 113 Chancery Lane, London WC2A 1PL (Ref. KG). Tel: 01-242 1222.
- The Law Society of Scotland, Legal Aid Central Committee, PO Box 123, 41 Drumsheugh Gardens, Edinburgh EH3 7YR. Tel: 031-226 7061.
- The Law Society of Northern Ireland, Legal Aid Department, RAC House, Chichester Street, Belfast BT1 4RR. Tel: 0232 246441.

All of these organizations produce leaflets about legal aid.

Choosing and dealing with lawyers

If you do decide to consult a lawyer about a consumer matter, it is very important that the lawyer you choose is experienced in handling your sort of case. Ask friends who have had similar problems what they thought of the solicitor they saw. You can also ask your local CAB, Consumer Advice Centre or Law Centre for a recommendation. Once the choice is made, sort out the financial side at an early stage, preferably at the time of making the appointment. If you want legal aid make this clear as not all lawyers will do legal aid work. If you want the fixed fee interview make this clear also as not all lawyers will do this either. If you are going to pay yourself then ask first what the solicitor charges. Fees vary considerably so you can shop around. Solicitors will not normally offer an all-in fee; they charge by the hour so ask what the hourly rate is. *Never* launch into a court case without first giving it serious thought and having a serious discussion with your solicitor about the costs of this. As the final figure will depend on how much time your lawyer has to spend on the case, the best they can do is to hazard a guess, but they should give you some idea of what you're letting yourself in for. If you win, the other side ought to be ordered to pay your legal costs but you lawyer might want to be paid more on top of that. Check this out! If you get legal aid, the legal aid fund might want you to reimburse them out of any damages you get for any costs which the other side haven't paid. If you lose the case, you could be ordered to pay the other side's costs, and this too needs thinking about.

Further information

An enormous amount has been printed on the subject of consumer rights. Practically every organization referred to in this book has produced a leaflet or booklet setting out who they are and what they do. Sometimes they provide these free to those who enquire and sometimes they demand a fee. If you want a leaflet about any organization or body mentioned here, you should approach them and request one. There are also lots of free advice leaflets available and these can be found in CABs, Consumer Advice Centres, local authority trading standards departments and libraries.

The Office of Fair Trading publishes several leaflets for the consumer and more detailed booklets for the benefit of traders. They publish a list of all their publications, stating which are free and giving the prices of those that are not. They will also provide leaflets direct if these are not available locally. Write to: The Office of Fair Trading, Room 310c, Field House, 15–25 Breams Buildings, London EC4A 1PR.

The Consumers Association publishes the magazine *Which?* The Association, which is independent and funded by consumers, tests various products and publishes the results in the magazine together with general information and advice about consumer affairs. If you want to subscribe, write to the Consumers Association, PO Box 44, Hertford SG14 1SH.

Bibliography

Handbooks for consumers
John Harries, *Consumers Know Your Rights*, 3rd edition, London: Longman Professional 1983 p. 248.

National Federation of Consumer Groups, *A Handbook of Consumer Law*, London: Hodder & Stoughton 1982, pp. 188.

Consumer books for lawyers

Ross Cranston, *Consumers and the Law,* 2nd edition, London: Weidenfeld & Nicolson 1984, pp. 560.

B.W. Harvey, *The Consumer Protection and Fair Trading*, 2nd edition, London: Butterworth 1982, pp. 452.

Robert Lowe and Geoffrey Woodroffe, *Consumer Law and Practice*, 2nd edition, London: Sweet & Maxwell 1985, pp. 459.

Consumer law encyclopedias

Francis Bennion, *Consumer Credit Control*, London: Longman Professional 1976.

Royston Miles Goode, *Consumer Credit Legislation*, London: Butterworth 1977.

W.H. Thomas (Ed.), *Encyclopedia of Consumer Law*, London: W. Green & Son, Sweet & Maxwell 1980.

Law in general (these can often be found in reference libraries)

J. Halsbury, *Halsbury's Laws of England*, London: Butterworth 1942.

J. Halsbury, *Halsbury's Statutes of England*, 4th edition, London: Butterworth 1985.

Stone's Justice Manual (Criminal Law), London: Butterworth, 1986.

Handbooks for businesspersons

John Harries, *Your Business and the Law*, 2nd edition, London: Longman Professional, 1983, p. 272.

13.

Taking action out of court

Consumers who are dissatisfied with a product or service can do a number of things which do not involve court proceedings. First and most obvious is to go back to the shop, etc., and complain. If that doesn't work, a complaint to some other body might do the trick. A consumer who still hasn't obtained redress might be tempted to take direct action or refuse to pay. If it appears there is no redress available some people might want to campaign for a change in the law. In this chapter we offer advice about all these possible courses of action.

Making a complaint

If traders or service persons have given you a bad service or done you a disservice such as leaving a patch of oil on the floor which you've slipped up on, or you have any other grievance against them and you want redress then you will inevitably have to confront them with the fact of their wrongdoing at some stage or other.

In the vast majority of cases it is best to let them know about your grievance as soon as possible. However, if the notification of your claim is likely to lead to the covering up of evidence (e.g. a hasty clean-up of the dirty kitchen after you write in and say you have food poisoning) or the intimidation of witnesses (e.g. the friendly shop-assistant who helped you to your feet after you fell in the patch of oil suddenly doesn't remember a thing after your letter of complaint has arrived and their employer has 'had a word'), then it might be best not to rush into it. In such cases it might be best to go straight to the trading standards department, for example, with your complaint or to make sure that either you or your adviser have got signed statements from witnesses before letting the transgressors know that you are after them.

If the case is serious, it is probably always best to let your adviser make the first approach but don't leave it too late. There are strict time limits within which legal actions must be started (three years in the case of personal injury), and no one will pay you anything once that limit has run out.

If it is not a serious case, nor one where evidence might be covered up or witnesses intimidated and you've decided to complain yourself, then you'll have to decide whether it would be better to make a personal visit first or to write.

Paying a visit

If possible take someone with you, both to give moral support and to act as a witness. This might be useful later if the visit isn't successful and you want to take the matter further. It is a good idea to visit at a time when a lot of other potential buyers are likely to be in the shop or service place. The sound of a vociferous complaint is likely to lose the trader a lot of business and s/he will be well aware of this.

Although it is not advisable to be rude straight away, particularly as you might be talking to an overworked or underpaid employee whose fault it definitely is not, be prepared to be forceful if necessary. Although some shops respond positively to customers' complaints others do not and may use tactics ranging from making the consumer feel rather silly to being downright offensive. Make sure you know what you want before you go in and then stick to your guns. Look at the sections that tell you what you are legally entitled to and then decide what lesser offer you would be prepared to accept. If you don't want to wait while the goods are sent back to the manufacturers to be put right, then say so. Don't forget that if the product or service is not up to scratch then you have been wronged. Demand your rights and don't let them get away with it.

Example Dialogue
Consumer 'I've brought this kettle back. I bought it here last week and it doesn't work.'
Shop person 'Oh, so what did you do to it then, love? Dropped it on the floor, I suppose.'
Consumer 'No. I haven't damaged it in any way. It simply doesn't work.'
Shop person 'OK. Tell you what I'll do. I'll send it back to the manufacturers for you.'

Consumer 'I'm not satisfied with that. Either you replace it on the spot or I want my money back.'

Shop person 'Sorry, love, can't do that. Has to go back to the manufacturers. OK?'

Consumer 'No, it's not OK. You have breached the provisions of the Sale of Goods Act by selling me a shoddy kettle which is not of merchantable quality, if you know what that means.'

Shop person 'No, I don't know what that means. Do you want me to send it back for you or not?'

Consumer 'I've already told you I don't. Either you give me another kettle or a refund. I know what my legal rights are.'

Shop person (sighing) 'All right then. Just this once. I just hope I don't get any more like you in today. I mean, I'll go out of business if this goes on.'

Writing a letter

If it's not possible to make a visit because the shop is a long way away or you are ill or, for example, you bought the goods by mail order, then you will have to write and complain instead. If you've visited and been fobbed off it might be a good idea to follow up with a letter. Observe the following:

- Keep a copy of the letter.
- Consider sending it by recorded delivery so you can prove you sent it. Some trading associations, for example, insist that you try and resolve matters with their member first. Proof that you sent a letter that has not been answered should suffice.
- Do not include any original documents. Send a photocopy and keep the original, otherwise your proof of purchase, for example, might mysteriously disappear.
- Make sure the letter goes to the right place. Some mail order companies, for example, have a special address for complaints.
- Quote any relevant reference number.
- Keep the letter short and to the point. Don't say anything in it that you might later wish to retract. If the matter ever goes to court the letter will have to be produced. (You can avoid the letter being produced if you write the words 'without prejudice' at the top of it.)

Include the following details:

- Date and place of purchase.
- How much you paid, plus a copy of the receipt if you have this.
- What is wrong with the item or service. If you're feeling brave, you can add why this is a breach of the law or of a code of ethics or practice.
- What redress you seek.
- A time limit within which you expect to receive redress, coupled with an assurance that you will take further action if nothing has happened by then. If you already know what you intend to do next then you can specify this, but it is not a good idea to threaten something and not do it. You must, however, give warning before taking court proceedings (see p. 201).

Taking the matter further

In all the sample letters below the aggrieved consumers have made it clear that if they do not receive satisfaction soon they will 'take the matter further.' One way of doing so which does not involve court proceedings is to report the offender to various persons who might use their influence to achieve an out of court settlement. The consumer's complaint could be made to a government department, the offender's trading association or ombudsman (if any), to their disciplinary body (if any) or to an organization which has recommended their products (if any) or by using a statutory complaints procedure where appropriate. Below we examine all these options.

Reporting them to the 'authorities'

The 'authorities' consist of officials who work for local authorities and at a national level the Office of Fair Trading. The latter is best communicated with via the medium of the former.

As mentioned already, all local authorities have departments which are concerned with the protection of the consumer. Throughout the book it has been stated that various types of bad behaviour by businesspersons are a criminal offence. The responsibility for bringing the offender to book lies with these local authority departments.* The departments also collect

---

* In Northern Ireland the job of enforcing the law lies with the Department of Commerce and in Scotland with the Procurator Fiscal.

1001 Blossom Buildings
London Z1

1 April 19__

Wheeler Auto Dealers
111 Zoom-zoom Lane
London Z1

For the attention of the manager

Dear Sir

On 30 May 19__ I purchased from your establishment a Honduki car, registration number XYZ 123P. I paid £450 for it and I enclose a copy of the
invoice.

Before I had decided to buy this car your employee Mr Nixon assured me that
it was in excellent condition, had been fully serviced and had nothing wrong
with it at all. If he had not said what he did I would not have bought the
car.

On 31 May 19__ I was driving the car along the M4 motorway when the engine
blew up. I called the AA who have towed the car back to my above address.

In the circumstances it is obvious that the statements made by Mr Nixon were
incorrect and that the car was not, when sold to me, of merchantable quality
as required by Section 14 of the Sale of Goods Act 1979. I am therefore
entitled to a complete refund of all the money I paid to you.

I therefore demand that without delay you return the entire £450 to me and
take the car away as I do not want it any more. If you do not give me my
money back within the next seven days then you may rest assured that I shall
take the matter further.

Yours faithfully

Wally Driver

Wally Driver

1002 Blossom Buildings
London Z1

1 April 19__

Gorgeoso Jumpers PLC
End of the World Lane
Townsley

Dear Gorgeoso Jumpers PLC

On 1 March 19__ I sent you a cheque for £15 in payment for a checked jumper
I had seen advertised, with illustration, in the 29 February edition of the
Daily Doings newspaper. I enclose a copy of the advertisement in question.

On 26 March 19__ I received a striped cardigan which your firm had sent me
by mistake. I do not want a striped cardigan and I return same to you
herewith.

I request that in accordance with your obligations under the British Code
of Advertising Practice you send me without delay a complete refund/a
checked jumper [decide which you want] plus the cost of posting the cardigan
back to you which is £1.

If I do not hear from you within the next seven days I shall take the matter
further.

Yours faithfully

Esmeralda Bloggs

Esmeralda Bloggs

2003 Blossom Buildings
London Z1

1 April 19___

Conner Radio Repairs
Waveband Road
Wavebandsville

Dear Conner Radio Repairs

Following my visit to your shop on 25 March 19___ I am writing to confirm these facts.

On 1 March 19___ I left my Sontachi Radio at your shop to be repaired. When I returned to collect it on 25 March 19___ your Mr Conner told me that it was now 'working perfectly' and then presented me with a bill for £20 (copy enclosed) which I paid.

When I got home I discovered that the radio was not in fact working at all and I returned at once to your shop. I spoke again to Mr Conner who refused either to do any further work on the radio without payment or to refund my money.

Under Section 13 of the Supply of Goods and Services Act 1982 you were under a duty to repair my radio with reasonable care and skill and this duty you have clearly breached. In the circumstances I demand the return of my £20.

If you do not return my money within the next seven days I shall take the matter further.

Yours faithfully

Helen Highwater

Helen Highwater

information about traders who persistently breach the civil law by, for instance, selling shoddy goods. If the behaviour of the trader in question is sufficiently bad, the trading standards officer might report him/her to the Office of Fair Trading.

If you consider that any trader has breached the criminal or civil law in their dealings with you then it is worth reporting them to your local authority. It is possible that the trading standards officer may be able to effect a 'friendly settlement'. If, on the other hand, the local authority decides to prosecute the trader this might work to your advantage because of the court's power to order that you be compensated (see p. 199). If the trader refuses to sort things out voluntarily or if no criminal offence has occurred, then you will have to try some other sort of action as trading standards officers do not involve themselves in civil court proceedings.

The Office of Fair Trading (Field House, 15–25 Breams Buildings, London EC4A 1PR) is headed by the Director General of Fair Trading and has various statutory duties and powers. It is funded by and responsible to central government. The OFT will not deal with individual complaints about such things as shoddy and misdescribed goods, but it does have specific powers to control the behaviour of traders and to prevent some from trading at all. We have already mentioned the way in which the Director is responsible for controlling the conduct of certain types of businesspersons, namely estate agents (see p. 94), hirers of goods (p. 121), sellers of credit (p. 128) and credit reference agencies. If a chorus of complaints reaches the OFT via trading standards officers then those that need licences to operate might have them taken away and estate agents can ultimately be banned from trading if they behave badly.

The Director also has a duty under the Fair Trading Act 1973 to take action against *any* trader who persists in conduct which is unfair to consumers. This includes conduct which breaches the criminal law, e.g. the Trade Descriptions Act, and conduct which breaches the civil law, e.g. the Sale of Goods Act. The Director collects information about bad behaviour by a trader and once the dossier is sufficiently damning s/he can demand that the trader in question gives an undertaking to desist in the future from the bad conduct complained of. Traders who refuse to give an undertaking or who give one which they later don't keep to can be taken to court. Once taken to court, the trader has a choice of giving another undertaking or being ordered to behave. Traders who later breach this undertaking to the court or disobey the court's order would then be in contempt of court for which they can be fined or sent to prison. None of the above can or will happen unless consumers voice their grievances.

Reporting them to a trading association or ombudsman

There are those who believe that private enterprise is best left to regulate its own affairs rather than being controlled by legislation. It has been suggested that from a consumer point of view such an attitude could be seen as fallacious. Be that as it may, various trading associations have been established which businesspersons can choose to join. Some trading associations have drawn up codes of practice with the blessing of the Office of Fair Trading which is under a statutory duty to encourage them in such activity. Members of the associations are supposed to abide by the rules of the code and risk expulsion if they do not do so. There are other trading associations which have rules for their members but no OFT approved code. There are also at present two ombudsmen schemes (for insurance and banking) whereby those organizations which have joined the scheme agree to let the ombudsman resolve disagreements and to be bound by the ombudsman's decision. There are other voluntary schemes too, such as those for the building trade and the newspaper scheme in respect of mail order advertisements. If such a scheme exists in respect of a consumer's grievance and if the offending trader has agreed to join it then, especially in the case of a small claim, it might be worth asking a trading association to intervene. This method of resolution could be easier, quicker and cheaper than going to court and below we set out some hints as to how to go about it.

To find out if there is a voluntary scheme of which you can take advantage, look under the relevant heading in this book and use the index. If the particular trade is covered here (and we don't have room to cover everything), you will find out what is available. New schemes are being set up all the time though, so it is worth getting advice to find out if the trade in question is now covered.

If you know there is a scheme, how can you find out whether the offending trader belongs to it? Many trading associations oblige their members to display the association symbol, so look in the shop or catalogue as appropriate. If you see nothing you could ask the trader direct or phone the association and ask if the trader has joined. If not, you'll have to forget this option and take up another.

If the erring personage is a member of a trading association, then you must complain direct to the trader before the trading association will listen to you. Some codes also insist that a complaint go the head office of the organization concerned. If, therefore, you have not yet written a letter of complaint then do so now (see p. 174) and keep a copy. Some trading associations encourage consumers to consult their trading standards officer, CAB or Consumer Advice Centre so consider this too if it is practicable and if you have not done so already.

Before actually complaining to a trade association it is worth trying to get hold of a copy of the code of practice (if any) in question so that you know exactly what the trader has agreed to do or not to do. Only some of the provisions of the codes are mentioned in this book. If you want to see the whole text of one then you could first try asking the trader for a copy as some codes insist that such be available for customers to peruse. Failing that you could ask the trading association to send you one but they may charge you for this. The OFT's free leaflets also summarize code of practice provisions.

When writing, specify who you are complaining about and why and enclose a copy of your letter of complaint to the trader in question. If you can, specify why what has happened is a breach of the code of practice and or the law and say what you want the trading association to do. Example letters are given below.

Having made your complaint then hopefully you will receive the redress you require. But what if you don't? What happens next depends on what the particular code says. Some provide as the next step another informal procedure sometimes referred to as 'conciliation'. This might involve putting the matter to a panel consisting of a variety of persons. In other cases the consumer might be offered the chance to send the offending item to a testing centre. In the latter case the consumer might have to pay a fee which might be refundable if the tester agrees later that the complaint was justified. If the fee is high, it might not be worth your while to do this so you might want to consider other options. If the conciliation procedure does not resolve the matter satisfactorily, some codes will give up and leave it to the consumer to go to court. Others offer the consumer the chance of arbitration. This is dealt with on p. 196. Don't agree to this without taking advice because by doing so you will invariably be giving up your right to go to court about the issue.

1001 Blossom Buildings
London Z1

1 May 19__

The Conciliation Service
Motor Agents Association Ltd

Dear Motor Agents Association Ltd

I am writing to request that you consider a complaint that I wish to lodge
against one of your members, namely Wheeler Auto Dealers, 111 Zoom-zoom Lane,
London Z1, who sold me a secondhand car which broke down the day after I
bought it. I enclose a copy of the letter of complaint I sent to them on
1 April 19__ and to which I have received no reply.

I consider that Wheeler Auto Dealers have breached their obligations to me
under Section 14 of the Sale of Goods Act and that they made material misrepresentations to me as set out in my letter to them. I note that such
behaviour is in breach of your code of practice and that, also in breach of
the code, I was not given a checklist regarding pre-delivery inspection and
known defects.

I therefore request your assistance to resolve this matter. I do not want
to keep the car in the circumstances. I am willing for Wheeler Auto Dealers
to come and collect it but I want all the money I paid them returned to me.

Yours faithfully

Wally Driver

Wally Driver

1002 Blossom Buildings
London Z1

1 May 19__

Advertising Manager
Daily Doings Newspaper
Dynamo Street
London WC2

Dear Advertising Manager

On 1 March 19__ in response to an advertisement in your newspaper (copy enclosed), I sent a cheque to Gorgeoso Jumpers PLC in payment for a checked jumper. On 26 March 19__ I received a striped cardigan which I returned to sender on 1 April 19__. I enclose a copy of the letter that I sent with it. I have not heard anything from Gorgeoso Jumpers in response to that letter.

I consider that Gorgeoso Jumpers have breached the provisions both of the British Code of Advertising Practice and of Section 13 of the Sale of Goods Act. On the page of your newspaper where I saw this advertisement there was a statement that you require all your advertisers to abide by the provisions of the code.

I am therefore writing to you to complain about what has occurred and to ask you to help me get my money back plus the cost of returning the cardigan to Gorgeoso Jumpers.

Yours faithfully

Esmeralda Bloggs

Esmeralda Bloggs

2003 Blossom Buildings
London Z1

1 May 19__

Secretary of the Association
RETRA

Dear Secretary

I am writing to request your assistance and to compain about the behaviour of one of your members, namely Conner Radio Repairs, Waveband Road, Wavesband-ville who charged me £20 to repair a radio and did not do the repair properly. I enclose a copy of the letter of complaint I sent to them on 1 April 19__ and to which I have received no reply.

I consider that Conner Radio Repairs have breached their obligations to me under Section 13 of the Supply of Goods and Services Act 1982 as set out in my letter to them and I seek your assistance to resolve this matter. I want either my £20 back or for Conner Radio Repairs to repair my radio properly with no extra charge to me.

Yours faithfully

Helen Highwater

Helen Highwater

Reporting them to their disciplinary body

Some professionals, e.g. doctors and lawyers, have disciplinary or professional bodies to which a consumer could consider complaining if dissatisfied with a service. Some of these bodies have been established by statute and have statutory duties to get rid of undesirables. Others have been set up by the profession itself. Whether or not a consumer would directly benefit from such a complaint depends on the range of matters in which the particular disciplinary body is prepared to involve itself. Some, for example, are concerned only to ensure that members who behave in an unethical way are removed from membership and are thus in some cases prevented from practising. Others are prepared to intervene, for example, in fee disputes in such a way as might benefit the consumer.

To find out if there is a disciplinary body relevant to your case, look in the relevant section of this book and use the index. We cannot cover all the professions here so if the one you are concerned about is not mentioned, take advice. The next thing to find out is whether the person you want to complain about is subject to such control. In the various sections we have pointed out that sometimes it is possible for a person to offer a professional service without having to be qualified and without therefore being subject to any control by a professional body. If, however, somebody pretends to be qualified when s/he is not, then the professional body may take action against him/her.

Would the disciplinary body deal with this particular issue? In the sections we have given an outline of some of the issues various disciplinary bodies are prepared to take up for aggrieved consumers and what matters they are prepared to investigate. Some of these bodies produce free information leaflets to guide consumers on this issue. If in doubt take advice or phone the organization concerned and ask them.

Have you explored all the avenues of complaint that you are supposed to have tried before complaining? For example, have you complained directly to the profession concerned, and in the case of NHS complaints, for example, is this a situation where you should use the NHS complaints procedure instead?

When making your complaint, identify who you are complaining about and why, and if possible pinpoint why the organization has a duty to deal with it. Say what you want them to do and what redress you seek.

Hopefully a letter of complaint will bring the desired result. If not, it may be possible to take the matter further still, either by arbitration or, for example in the case of solicitors, by complaining to an outside body about the way in which the complaint was handled.

Using a statutory complaints procedure

In the case of nationalized industries, the Health Service and government departments, there are complaints procedures established by statute which can be utilized by the consumer. These consist of consultative councils and ombudsmen. If a consumer is dissatisfied with a public service it is well worth considering using a complaints procedure rather than going to court. If a complaint is accepted as being justified then the matter should be resolved without the necessity of court proceedings. Consider the following before starting the complaint off:

- Is there a procedure you could use? Look at relevant sections in this book and use the index. If in doubt take advice.
- Is it premature to complain? Have you taken the matter up with the local office, etc? See individual sections.
- Don't leave it too late to complain either. There are time limits, for example, for ombudsmen schemes (see individual sections).
- Some nationalized industries, e.g. gas, electricity and the Post Office, have drawn up codes of practice. Try and get hold of one and see what they have promised to do or not to do. Ask at your local showrooms or contact the consultative committee (address on bill).

When writing say why you are complaining and if possible (and if applicable), why what has happened is a breach of the code of practice. Detail what complaints you have made so far and to whom. Hopefully a written complaint will resolve the matter. If not, some codes provide for arbitration. (See later, and remember that if you agree to this you will not be able to go to court as well.) Alternatively, there might be a possibility of referral to the ombudsman. If there is nothing else you can do then take advice about court proceedings. It is possible to sue a nationalized industry. Recently a consumer was threatened with the sanction of having her electricity cut off it she did not pay a bill for damage to

3001 Blossom Buildings
London Z1

1 April 19__

The Secretary
Professional Purposes
The Law Society
8 Breams Buildings
London EC4 1HP

Dear Secretary

I wish to make a complaint about a firm of solicitors namely Twister, Turner
and Co., 111 Seedy Lane, Seedly. My complaint is as follows:

On 1 November 19__ I consulted Mr Stonewall, a partner in that firm, concerning injuries I had sustained in a road accident on 15 August 19__.
Mr Stonewall told me that he would require £500 on account of costs before he
would take the case on and I gave him a cheque for that amount. He then said
he would make the necessary investigations and negotiate with the other
driver's insurance company on my behalf. Since that discussion I have heard
nothing from him at all. I have written to him ten times and on the last
occasion I told him I would report him to the Law Society if he did not
answer. I have also telephoned him repeatedly and have been told on each
occasion that he is unavailable.

Please investigate this matter. Mr Stonewall has persistently delayed in
answering my letters and you do state in your leaflet that you will investigate such a matter. I am also concerned about what has happened to my money
which I would like returned as I now want to consult another solicitor. I
have made that clear in my last five letters to Mr Stonewall.

You have my permission to show a copy of this letter to Mr Stonewall.

Yours faithfully

Ivor Case

Ivor Case

her meter, damage which the consumer did not accept responsibility for. The consumer obtained a High Court injunction forbidding the cut off until the issue of who should pay was sorted out. The Electricity Board then backed down. (Blanchard v LEB (1985) J.M. Bowyer barrister)

Products with a mark of approval

A consumer may have brought a product because it had the mark of approval of some outside institution attached to it. In such a case it may be worth reporting the offender to that institution if dissatisfied. Below we give brief details of two particular such organizations.

The British Standards Institution

The 'kitemark' and 'safety mark,' hallmarks of approval by the British Standards Institution will probably be familiar to many consumers. The Institution sets 'British Standards' for a wide variety of products and in some cases manufacturers must manufacture their products in accordance with the standard set in order to be able to market the product lawfully. (Examples of products controlled in such a way are motorcycle crash helmets and car seatbelts.) Manufacturers can make a claim that their product complies with a British Standard but this does not mean that the BSI has checked up on them. In fact it is only where the kitemark or safety mark is displayed that the consumer can be assured that the BSI back the manufacturer's claim that the product in question does adhere to their set standards. If a consumer has a complaint about a product marked in this way which cannot be resolved with the manufacturer or retailer, then the consumer can complain further to BSI's Certification and Assessment Department at BSI, Maylands Avenue, Hemel Hempstead, Herts. Tel: 0442 3111. They will test the product and if they agree the product is not actually up to their standards they say they will assist in resolving the issue. The Institute will not actually intervene in other cases but they say they will always be interested to hear of consumer complaints about goods which manufacturers claim comply with British Standards. Further information about the Institute can be obtained from their Public Relations Department, BSI, 2 Park Street, London W1A 2BS. Tel: 01-629 9000.

The Design Council

Products with a 'Design Centre' label are likely to sell well. The Design Council, which bestows such labels on selected products, is sponsored by the government with the aim of encouraging and publicizing good British design. The Design Council say they will consider 'seriously' any complaints made about products with a Design Centre label. The manufacturer will be informed and the product could be reassessed and removed from the Design Centre selection. As the latter might have an adverse affect on sales this is an option worth considering.

The Design Council is at 28 Haymarket, London SW1Y 4SU, and there are Design Centres in London, Glasgow and Cardiff.

Direct action

If a visit or letter or complaint is of no avail consumers might be tempted to take direct action. This could consist of refusing to leave the premises, protesting outside the premises or elsewhere, ringing up the local newspaper or, where it is not too late, withholding payment.

Refusing to leave the premises

If your requests for redress are not heeded, it is tempting to say loudly: 'I refuse to leave until you refund my money!' This might have the desired effect, but what if it doesn't? What can they do to you?

They can of course ask you to leave. If you refuse then legally you become a trespasser with no right to remain. Trespassers cannot, as is popularly believed, be prosecuted (except in limited circumstances not applicable here) but they can be ejected by means of physical force provided no more force than is reasonable is used. Leave at once if this appears imminent. As you have no right to stay you have no legal right to take action to defend yourself against being removed and if it comes to fisticuffs you could be prosecuted for assault. If unreasonable force is used the consumer could sue for damages in the civil court or go to the local magistrates court and ask that a summons for assault be issued. If serious injuries result the police should be told, but they are unlikely to be interested otherwise.

The shop-owner could call the police if you refuse to leave. If so, the wisest thing to do is to make a dignified retreat. Provided no criminal offence has been committed the police cannot actually arrest you, but they could decide to assist the shop-owner in your removal. Resistance could lead to trouble!

The shop-owner has the theoretical right to sue for damages in the civil court if anyone trespasses on his/her property. However, once the protesting consumer has been removed s/he will probably lose interest in the entire affair.

Protesting outside the shop

You may consider a protest outside the shop either following eviction or after careful planning. If evicted after a complaint in the shop, don't stay outside shouting particularly if the police have been involved. You will very likely be arrested, e.g. for obstructing the highway or the police or for threatening words or behaviour likely to cause a breach of the peace.

Even if a quiet and carefully planned protest is later made outside the shop the weight of the law both civil and criminal may well descend. The risk of being arrested for obstruction or threatening words or behaviour still exists. The shop-owner can in theory also sue for damages for all or one of the following:

- Nuisance i.e. wrongful interference with the use of property.
- Conspiracy. It is a crime to conspire to commit a criminal offence and also a civil wrong to combine with others with the express purpose of injuring someone's 'legitimate interests', e.g. his/her business or trade.
- Defamation. This is the publication of a statement which reflects on a person's reputation so as to lower him/her in the eyes of 'right thinking' members of the public. If the statement is spoken it is called slander, if it is written, e.g. on a placard, it is called libel. Such an action can be defended on the basis that the words spoken or written were true but libel actions are expensive both to take and to defend.

Faced with a continuing protest outside a shop, a shop-owner could start off a legal action on one or other of the above grounds and ask for an immediate injunction to halt the protests meanwhile.

- Local people objected to the gentrification of their area and the resultant removal by fair means or foul of tenants in the private rented sector. They mounted a picket outside a local estate agents' for limited periods with small groups of people who had placards and distributed leaflets. The estate agents started a legal action against them claiming damages for nuisance, libel and conspiracy but they asked the court for an immediate injunction to clear the protesters from their doors. This was granted by the court. (Hubbard v Pitt 1976 QB 142)

Protesting away from the shop

A consumer who has been prevented from making an on-the-spot protest might consider making one elsewhere. Be warned that placing non-washable graffiti on someone else's property could lead to prosecution for criminal damage. Putting up a notice of protest might result in a libel action (see above) and a request for an immediate injunction. Although readers can take heart from the case quoted below, it should be remembered that even if an injunction were not granted, as in that case, if an intrepid trader pursued the matter to the bitter end and won, the hapless consumer could still be faced with a large bill for damages. It is probably best to take advice before publishing your rude remarks.

■ Partners in a house refurbishing business bought some paint to paint the outside of a house they were working on. The paint was trademarked 'Carsons' and was labelled 'Vandyke Brown'. Six months after the painting, the Vandyke Brown, to quote the trial judge, 'started to turn green in places and at the present day it certainly presents a multicoloured appearance not unlike military camouflage'. In revenge the partners put up a sign near the offending paintwork which read: 'This house is painted with Carsons paint.' The house was conveniently situated near a busy through road and, as the judge put it, the sign 'commanded a wide section of the reading public'. The partners were sued for trade libel and, amusingly, for infringement of the trademark. An immediate injunction was applied for to make them take the sign down but this the judge refused to grant. (Bestobell Paints Ltd v Bigg (1975) FSR 421)

Use of the media

An aggrieved consumer might consider contacting the various consumer periodicals or programmes on the television or radio or seeing if a newspaper would be interested in publicizing the injustice suffered. None of these will want to be sued for libel either so you would have to be sure of your facts and able to prove them. Trial by newspaper is not allowed so if a court case has been started the media are severely restricted in what they can report. The *Sunday Times* found this a considerable problem when they were trying to publish information about the plight of the Thalidomide victims (see p. 36). Also, the media being what it is, the story will have to be newsworthy.

Refusing to pay

Sometimes it is too late to consider this option. However, if a consumer has agreed, for instance, to pay only after a service has been performed, or if payment was made by cheque or credit agreement, it may be tempting if things go wrong to withhold or stop payment. Below we point out the possible pitfalls in doing so.

If you refer back to *Legal explanation* you will see that a consumer who enters into a binding contract cannot set that contract aside completely and claim a full refund unless an important term in the contract has been breached. If a less important term has been violated and the case goes to court, the consumer would only be entitled to damages. It follows that a consumer is not justified in refusing *all* payment if a minor breach of contract has taken place and doing so without legal justification could create trouble in the future. As a general principle, therefore, if the breach of contract is of the minor variety you should pay what you accept you owe and write to the trader stating why you are withholding the balance. If a major breach of contract has occurred then you are entitled to withhold all payment but once again a letter of explanation should be sent. If court proceedings are then threatened, if possible take advice, see p. 217.

Payment by cheque is a separate and legally enforceable promise by you to pay and you are only entitled to stop payment if what you got in return had absolutely no value at all. If this is not the case, stopping a cheque is not a good idea as you can be sued on that basis alone. If you backed the cheque with a cheque card the bank would not let you stop it anyway.

If you paid by credit in circumstances where the provider of credit is legally liable for any breaches of contract by the seller or service person, or if those persons provided the credit themselves, then it could be a good tactic to stop paying. However, as with cash purchases, it is not advisable to withhold all payment if a minor breach of contract has occurred. It is probably best to take advice before stopping payment, and advice should certainly be taken if you are served with a default notice. If, though, you obtained a 'no strings' loan (see p. 154) you are not entitled to stop paying because your agreement with the lender was separate and the fact that you used the money to pay for shoddy goods or services is not the legal responsibility of the lender.

Campaigning for change

A consumer who discovers that there is no legal or other redress available to compensate for a wrong suffered may wish to do something about this. If a law needs changing then strictly speaking it is up to the government ministry concerned with that particular subject to draw up the necessary legislation and lay it before Parliament. They might have to draw up a new Act of Parliament or just Regulations (see *Legal explanation*, p. 3). The ministry most concerned with consumer affairs is the Department of Trade and Industry (DTI) which deals, amongst other things, with consumer safety, consumer credit, trading standards and weights and measures. It is also responsible for the Office of Fair Trading, the National Consumer Council and various other consumer-orientated bodies, e.g. the nationalized industries' consumer councils. The DTI has a Special Consumer Safety Unit. If this Unit heard from a trading standards officer (they do not as a rule deal with the public direct) of a product that might be dangerous and was not covered by legislation, they would consider drafting the necessary legislation to cover the gap in the law and they might well take the issue up direct with the suppliers. They also are involved with setting safety standards (see p. 188) and in doing safety research.

The Office of Fair Trading (which concerns itself with economic matters) does have a statutory duty to collect information about the conduct of those commercial activities in the UK which relate to goods and services supplied to consumers and which might adversely affect the economic interests of UK consumers or their interests in respect of health, safety or other matters. This is stated in the Fair Trading Act 1973. The Director must also put this information to good use and advise the powers-that-be about legislation that should be introduced to protect consumers' interests.

There are other government ministries with responsibilities in areas which might concern consumers. The Home Office, for instance, deals with explosives, firearms, dangerous drugs and poisons. The Department of Health and Social Security covers the

NHS and medical products. The Ministry of Agriculture, Fisheries and Food, together with the DHSS, deals with food, i.e. what's in it, additives, etc., labelling and advertising. In Scotland the Scottish Home and Health Department deals with food matters and in Northern Ireland the Department of Commerce deals with consumer protection and weights and measures.

The EEC also has a consumer protection department. We have mentioned the role of the EEC in British law-making (see *Legal explanation*, p. 3). There are draft directives now being considered about doorstep selling and consumer credit. At the moment only doorstep credit transactions can be cancelled after a period of reflection and the EEC would like to see this extended to cover cash transactions as well. The EEC has recently passed directives about misleading advertising and manufacturers' liability for their products (see p. 37). These directives must be introduced into our law within prescribed time limits.

Campaigning

If a consumer thinks that the law needs changing there are a number of avenues which can be used to convey this opinion to those with the power to do something about it.

Trading standards officers are supposed to pass on information about wrongs done to the consumer. Whether anything would happen as a result of an individual complaint would no doubt depend on the seriousness of the incident and or on how many other people had complained about the same thing. Hence the advantage of communicating with other consumers, as emphasized below.

Your local MP is a good person to consider contacting. Ministries are far more likely to take notice of your complaint if it is passed on to them by an MP.

The National Consumer Council, (18 Queen Anne's Gate, London SW1H 9AA. Tel: 01-222 9501 – there are special consumer councils for Wales, Scotland and Northern Ireland) was established with the object (to quote their leaflet) of giving a 'vigorous and independent voice to consumers in the UK'. The Council is funded by the government but states that it is independent despite this. The Council is not expected to give advice to individuals about their consumer problems but to articulate the collective consumer cause to the government and others. The Council also campaigns for improvements in the position of the consumer by encouraging needed legislation and voluntary controls, and by trying to ensure that consumers are better informed and have access to free advice. The Council has special responsibilities towards inarticulate and disadvantaged consumers and to ensure effective consumer representation in the nationalized industries. The fact that the Council represents consumers as a whole and not individuals serves to emphasize the next point.

If you really do want to achieve change then try if possible not to go it alone. Unless you are very brave, determined articulate and sure of yourself you are likely to get discouraged and give up at an early stage. Also, on your own you don't carry much clout. It is easy to ignore the complaints of one person but not so easy to push aside an organized group. If you campaign as part of or with the assistance of a consumer pressure group or with the help of an advice agency you are far more likely to succeed in your objectives.

14.

Courts and arbitration

If a consumer's complaints fail then the matter can only be resolved by arbitration or court proceedings. Some trading associations offer out-of-court arbitration or the consumer could sue the trader in the County Court, where the case could also be referred to arbitration. In addition, if the local authority were to prosecute the trader in the criminal courts the consumer might be awarded compensation.

Out-of-court arbitration

If a friendly settlement is not on offer and a criminal prosecution not possible, then another option which might be available to the consumer, instead of going to court, is to agree to arbitration. This is a method of resolving the dispute in a way that is legally binding without the necessity of either party having to go to court. If possible, and particularly in a case where more than a few pounds are at stake, take advice before agreeing to this procedure because it is invariably an alternative to going to court. You are not usually allowed to do both and you will be stuck with the arbitrator's decision whether you like it or not (unless they were to do something absolutely outrageous).

As will be seen later (p. 201), if a consumer does take a small claim to the county court it too can be dealt with by a procedure called arbitration. We are not concerned with that procedure here but with out-of-court arbitrations which are frequently offered by trading associations, etc. as a last resort method of deciding a dispute between one of their members and a consumer. (Look under particular headings to see whether arbitration may be available in your case.) If arbitration is available then it will usually involve the following stages.

First, both sides must agree to the arbitration. You might find you'd already 'agreed' to it when you signed the original contract, but usually you will be sent a simple form to fill in saying that you agree. At the same time you will probably be asked to pay a registration fee. If you win, the arbitrator will have a discretion to make the other side refund this to you or you could be made to forfeit it if you lose. At the moment the fee charged by the Institute mentioned below is £17.25 for claims up to £2,500 (although individual schemes may provide a lesser amount). You should have a copy of the rules that will apply to the arbitration before you agree to it. If not, demand a copy and read what they say!

Who will arbitrate? Many codes of practice require that you agree that the person be chosen by the Chartered Institute of Arbitrators. The Institute is an independent body which promotes and facilitates the determination of disputes by arbitration. It operates special small-claim consumer arbitrations besides its other work which can involve it in large commercial disputes on a worldwide basis. The Institute is based at the International Arbitration Centre, 75 Cannon Street, London EC4N 5BH. Tel: 01-236 8761.

The Institute's procedure provides that the consumer gets a claim form to fill in (in duplicate) which must be returned completed to the Institute within 28 days of its receipt. On the form you will be asked to give a summary of your complaints. As arbitrators apply principles of law it is probably worth specifying, if you can, what rules of law have been breached especially as you will not be present (see later). You will also be asked to specify what amount of compensation you are claiming and to include (also in duplicate) copies of any supporting documents (see example claim). This will be regarded as your full and final claim and you will not be allowed to later ask for more except with permission, which you might not get.

Next the Institute sends a copy of your completed claim form and supporting documents to the trader who must then, within 28 days of receipt, send in their written defence and any supporting documents. All of these will then be sent to you. You then have 14 days to send (in duplicate) your written comments on what has been said in the defence. You cannot raise any new issues at this point but you should state what parts of the traders arguments you do not agree with and why. Also, if the trader has omitted to comment on a point raised by you, you should state this and request that they do answer.

The arbitrator then looks at the documents and makes a

decision. There will be no oral hearing. (If there was it would cost you a lot more and might render the whole exercise non cost-effective.) A copy of the decision with the reasons for it will be sent to you.

If you have won, you should get your money within 21 days. However, in the unlikely event of the trade association member not paying up, the award is enforceable through the courts as if it were a court judgement. (See p. 212 for how this system works.)

When comparing this sort of arbitration with one in the County Court you will note when you've read the section about the latter that the court fee to start the case off is less than the registration fee for the smaller claims. At a certain point, the court gets more expensive and also the possible penalties for losing in court are higher. The court's procedures, although they do try and simplify them for small claims, are probably still more difficult to cope with but the consumer does have the luxury of an oral hearing.

Summary of complaints

■ On 1 March 19___ I took my Sontachi radio to Conner Radio Repairs, Waveband Road, Wavesbandville because it had ceased to work and was making no sound at all. I saw a man called Mr Conner in the shop. He agreed that the shop would repair the radio for me and he gave me a receipt for it. I called in several times as he told me the radio would be ready in a few days. On 25 March 19___ Mr Conner returned the radio to me and took the receipt from me. He told me the radio was now 'working perfectly' and asked me to pay his bill of £20 which I did by cheque. I went home and plugged the radio in. It made no noise at all. I immediately went back to the shop and complained. Mr Conner accused me of damaging the radio myself and said that this was why the radio did not work. He refused to do any further work on it without charge or to give me a refund. I did not damage the radio in any way.

It is my case that Conner Radios have breached Section 13 of the Supply of Goods and Services Act 1982 in that they have not repaired my radio using reasonable care and skill.

In this case the consumer, Highwater, should include in duplicate if she has them copies of the bill and, if payment is disputed, proof that she did pay and copies of all correspondence between herself and Mr Conner. If anyone witnessed what happened in the shop or can say that she did not damage the radio herself, she should include signed letters from them.

Note that Ms Highwater could have started this case off in the county court for only £7 (present fees). However, if she is too busy to bother with the county court procedures and doesn't want to go to a hearing, this may be a better course of action for her.

Criminal prosecution

If a consumer reports a trader to the local trading standards officer then the latter may decide to prosecute. Obviously what has occurred must amount to a breach of the criminal law before this can be considered. (See individual sections and use index to see if this applies to your situation.) Has the product or service been falsely described, for example? If so, this may be a breach of the Trade Descriptions Act. Has someone been injured? If so, the product might not comply with a safety regulation.

If a prosecution is to be brought then it is up to the local authority to do so and not the aggrieved consumer, so you will not have the bother of preparing court papers nor will you have to pay any court fees. If the prosecution is successful (and the case will have to be proven beyond all reasonable doubt) then, in addition to any sentence meted out to the offending trader, the court might also order the trader to pay an amount of compensation to the consumer. If this occurs it will be up to the criminal court to make sure the offender pays up. All this makes this option quite attractive but there are limitations:

- The prosecution would take place in either the magistrates' court (sheriffs' court in Scotland) or in the Crown Court (High Court in Scotland) depending on the seriousness of the matter. The particular relevance to the consumer is that the Crown Court can award unlimited amounts of compensation (and can pass higher sentences). The most the magistrates can award is £2,000 per offence charged. Offences can be what is called 'taken into consideration' and compensation can be ordered in respect of those matters too, but the maximum overall cannot exceed £2,000 per offence charged.
- Compensation can only be ordered in respect of personal injury, loss or damage which has resulted because of the commission of the offence charged. The causal link must be clear.

- The court will only make a compensation order if the issues are clear and simple. If the case is complex the court will leave the consumer to sue the trader in the civil court.
- If death has resulted or if losses have occurred following a road accident then compensation cannot be awarded in a criminal court.
- The court will not order someone to pay compensation if that person obviously has no means to pay. In the case of traders who are still in business this is unlikely to apply.

If a criminal prosecution does take place then make sure your trading standards officer knows that you want to be awarded compensation. This is particularly important in Scotland. Make sure too that you have provide him/her with the necessary proof of your loss, e.g. an up-to-date medical report in the case of injuries or the sales invoice if you want a refund in the case of goods. If you have time then consider attending the court hearing so that if any query about the compensation crops up you can answer it. You will not be asked to attend if the trader is pleading guilty or if your evidence is not disputed. You can still choose to go despite this, but you will not be awarded any costs of attending in this event. Do not be afraid to leap up in the public gallery and make your presence known if necessary, e.g. if the local authority forgets to mention that you want to be compensated.

If an award is made the offender will either be ordered to pay it all within a specified time limit or will be allowed to pay by instalments. If they do not do so then the court ought to summon them and demand an explanation. They might then be given another chance to pay but the ultimate result of not paying is prison and so it follows that most traders will pay up. The consumer does not have to play any part in the enforcement process. It should happen automatically but if your money doesn't come through when it should have done, don't be afraid to ring up the court and ask what has happened.

Going to court

If all else fails a consumer who wants redress will have to take his/her case to the civil court. However, there is no need to be dismayed on this account. Taking someone else to court over a small sum may be time-consuming but it is not actually difficult nor need it be prohibitively expensive. Courts are often thought of as intimidating places but in fact going to a civil court over a small claim should not be at all frightening. All you need is the confidence to do it yourself.

Whatever you do, don't leave it too long. There are time limits within which court actions must be commenced. Claims for personal injury or death must be brought within three years. That might sound like a long time but you will be suprised how quickly the years go by. Claims for economic loss can be brought within six years.

Before you start any court case off you must first write to the trader warning that court proceedings will be started against them if they do not pay up. The court might disallow your costs if they felt you had not done everything possible to effect an out-of-court settlement.

The courts

In England and Wales, cases where less than £5,000 is being claimed are dealt with in the County Court. If the sum claimed is less than £500 then the court will deal with the case by the arbitration procedure which is held in private. (Only in exceptional circumstances will the court not deal with the matter in this way.) If more than £500 is claimed the case can still be dealt with by arbitration but only if the court and both sides agree. Other claims are heard in open court before a judge. Claims of over £5,000 are dealt with in the High Court. Never launch into this without advice!

In Scotland civil claims are heard in the Sheriffs' Court. There is no arbitration scheme but claims not exceeding £1,000 can be dealt with under the summary cause procedure which is simpler than the procedure in other cases.

In Northern Ireland civil claims under £5,000 are dealt with in the County Court. There is an arbitration scheme but only for claims not exceeding £300. Disputed claims for sums between £300 and £500 are dealt with by a court official called a registrar. Registrars can also deal with undisputed claims of up to £1,000. Other County Court cases are heard by a judge. Claims exceeding £5,000 go to the High Court.

Is it worth going to court?

This depends partly on what chance you have of winning, what you stand to lose if you don't win and whether you will get your money if you do win.

The chance of winning

In civil cases the person who makes the claim has to establish that s/he is in in legal right on 'the balance of probabilities'. If therefore the weight of evidence is equal on both sides the trader will probably get away with it. But if consumers can just manage to tip the scales in their favour they will win. This contrasts with the situation in the criminal court where the prosecution must prove its case beyond all reasonable doubt, a much higher onus to discharge. How can you tell if you are going to tip the scales in your favour or not? Sometimes it may be perfectly obvious that the consumer is in the right and the other side's failure to pay up may be the result of sheer inefficiency or the hope that the consumer will give up when faced with a wall of silence. The fictional claim against Gorgeoso Jumpers might be an example of such a situation. All a consumer needs to worry about in such a case is whether the erring trader has got any money left (see later). In other cases it may be obvious that the other side are up, for a fight and will not give in. Take the fictional claim (see above) against Conner Radios, for example. Mr Conner might allege that when Ms Highwater brought the radio back she confessed to him that it worked all right until she dropped it. In his position as a professional radio repairer he might be able to discourse in a learned fashion about the workings of radios to his own advantage. In such a situation and if there are no witnesses it will be his word against hers. Unless Ms Highwater can get a person knowledgeable about radios to contradict Mr Conner she might not win. If in doubt about your chances try to take advice.

Will you get your money if you do win?

You cannot get blood out of a stone. If a person you want to sue has no money at all or if a company has gone out of business then you will not benefit out of suing them. If the person or outfit you want to sue is in business they may be trading as a company, as a sole trader or as a partnership. (Partnerships are groups of people trading together who have not formed a company.) If the outfit is a company you can only get at the company's assets and not at the possessions of the individuals within it (unless they have behaved fraudulently). Once a company has gone into liquidation, they're not usually worth suing. If you think this is a possibility you can do what is called a company search. You can do this by going to the Companies Regstration Office, London Search Room, Companies House, 55–71 City Road, London EC1Y 1BB. The fee is £1 and they are open 9.30–4.30 Alternatively, you can do a postal search. Write to the Companies Registration Office, Crown Way, Maindy, Cardiff CF3UZ, sending a cheque for £3 made payable to the Registrar of Companies. Or you can pay a Company Registration Agent or Law Agent to do the search for you (look in *Yellow Pages*).

In the case of non-company traders, you can get at the assets both of the business and of the trader and his/her partners. You should be able to find out who they are because all persons (and companies) who are trading under a name which is not their own, e.g. 'Wheeler Auto Dealers', are legally obliged to state their real names on all correspondence, orders and invoices and they should display a notice with their real names on it at their business premises. This is stated in the Business Names Act 1985 (except in Northern Ireland where there is a regulation to cover this). If an individual owns a house s/he is always worth suing. If s/he has the capital you will in the end be able to get at it; if s/he has a salaried job you could get a court order against this salary. If an individual has valuable possessions which they own outright the court can make an order that these things be sold to pay you. If a trader is still trading there should be something on their premises which could be taken to pay you back!

What do you stand to lose if you don't win?

Before starting the case off you will have to pay a court fee, which will not be returned to you if you lose. Also, if you lose you will nearly always be ordered to pay the other side's costs. Costs consist of their lawyers fees (but see below), the fees of their witnesses for attending court and expenses they incurred in obtaining such things as photographs and expert reports. The court does limit how much they are allowed to charge in respect of all these items. For example £38 a day maximum is usually allowed to an expert witness even though some 'experts' would probably want much more than that. Also, the expense must have been necessarily incurred and relevant to the case.

If an arbitration hearing takes place in England or Wales then the losing party cannot be ordered to pay for the other person's lawyer. If an arbitration takes place in Northern Ireland then losing parties will be made to forfeit only their court fee unless the arbitrator considers they have behaved unreasonably.

Getting the show on the road

If you do decide to take the plunge and go to court what can you expect? In the following pages we will trace the path of a small County Court action in England and Wales. Unfortunately there is not space to do the same for Scotland and Northern Ireland but the procedures are broadly the same although in Scotland particularly, different legal names and terms are used to denote what are essentially the same things. You can obtain information about small claims in Scotland from a free booklet called *Guide to the New Summary Cause in the Sheriff Court* from Sheriffs' Courts or Citizens Advice Bureaux. For Northern Ireland see *Small Claims in Northern Ireland* by D.S. Greer (SLS Legal Publications (Northern Ireland), 2nd edition, 1982). In England and Wales there is a free booklet available at County Courts called *Small Claims in the County Court* which contains more information than we have room for here.

Before starting off a court case in England and Wales there are some preliminary matters to be considered.

Which court?

It is important to start the case off in the right County Court. You can either use the court for the area where the defendant lives or carries on his/her business or the court for the area where the 'cause of action' arose. To use the examples quoted above, Mr Driver will sue Wheeler Auto Dealers in the court for London Z1. That is where they carry on business and the contract, breach of which gives rise to his claim, was struck in the same place. Ms Highwater will sue Conner Radio Repairs in the Wavesbandville County Court for the same reason even though she lives in London Z1. Ms Bloggs will sue Gorgeoso Jumpers either in the Townsley County Court or, more conveniently for her, in the London Z1 court. This is because the contract in that case was concluded when she posted her cheque. (Mail order is difficult, so ring up the court or take advice when in doubt.) If you do not know where the relevant court is, look in the phone book under 'Courts' and if you don't know whether the location is in that court's catchment area ring them up and ask.

Which defendant?

This sounds simple but sometimes it isn't. You must also have an address for them. Companies are regarded as separate legal entities so if dealing with an outfit that puts Ltd or PLC after its name you sue that name and the address you give to the court must be their registered office, not an address which they might be trading from. The location of the registered office should by law be printed on all their stationery but if for some reason you do not know what it is you can find out by doing a company search (see p. 202). In the Gorgeoso Jumpers case therefore, the defendant will be Gorgeoso Jumpers PLC. If the trader is not a company but a partnership (see p. 202) you can sue them in their trade name adding the words '(A Firm)'. If the proposed defendant is a sole trader you can sue him/her in his/her own name adding '(Trading as —)', giving the trade name and the trade address.

Having sorted these matters out you are now ready to go. To actually start the case off you must fill in various forms and pay the court a fee. This can be done by post but if possible call in at the court and do it all on the spot. Although the procedure is not actually difficult there are lots of petty mistakes you could make, in which case the court documents will go backwards and forwards between you and the court staff until everything is sorted out. The amount of the fee depends on the amount of the claim. At the moment, there is a minimum charge of £7. Otherwise, for claims up to £300 the fee is 10p for every £1 or part of claimed. For claims of between £300 and £500 the fee is £37 and for claims between £500 and £2,000 it is £43. You will get this fee back if you win. There are two sorts of form to be completed. One is called the 'Particulars of Claim' where you set out what your case is all about. The other form is called a 'Request' form in which you ask the court to issue a summons calling the defendant to account.

The particulars of claim

If you decide to go to the court to start the case off it is worth preparing at least a draft of these before you go. You can type or write them out yourself or fill out a form which you can get from the court. The court will want one copy for themselves and one per defendant (carbons are not allowed) and you should keep one for yourself. Use A4 paper if doing your own and set it out like the examples below. Call yourself the plaintiff and the person you are suing the defendant (pursuer and defender in Scotland). When stating your case the court will not be too fussy with a small claim but it is important to get certain points across. Just stick to the facts and keep it short and to the point. Make the points one by one and in numbered paragraphs. Include the following:

1. If the defendant is a trader, open by stating that fact and naming them and the nature and place of their business. (This is

important because businesspersons have greater responsibilities in respect of shoddy goods, etc. than do private persons.)
2. Identify the deal. State where it took place, when it took place what it consisted of and what the price and other conditions were, e.g. time of delivery. (See the examples below.)
3. Identify the wrong you suffered. (See examples again.)
4. State what redress you seek. There could be three elements in this.
   (a) Return of money paid for goods retained.
   (b) Damages (see *Legal explanation*).
   (c) Interest. This can be claimed from the date the bad behaviour occurred up to the judgement day. If you don't ask for it you won't get it, but you will have to do some calculations so it is up to you if you can be bothered. Ask the court what rate you can claim.
   (d) Costs (see p. 203).
5. If the claim is more than £500 state, if this is so, that you want the case to go the arbitration.

The Request Form

The court will provide this form. They will want only one copy of it completed but it might be a good idea to keep a copy of it for yourself. The form consists of a number of questions which you have to fill in the answers to. At first these questions may look confusing, hence the advantage of going to the court and filling it all in there. In fact all you are being asked is your name and address, who you are suing and their address, a one sentence statement of what the claim is about, how much it is for and confirmation that because of the circumstances it is in the catchment area of that County Court.

What happens next

Once all the forms have been sorted out and the fee paid the court will give the case a number which must be cited on all future occasions and you will be given a piece of paper called a 'plaint note'. Do not lose it or confusion will follow.

The court then posts several forms, including your Particulars of Claim, to the opposition. They are supposed to state on one form whether they admit you are in the right and if not why not. If they do agree they ought to pay up, they should state how much they agree to pay and when. You have to decide whether to accept this offer or not. The trader should fill in the form and return it to

IN THE LONDON Z1 COUNTY COURT   Case No..(see later)

BETWEEN

                        ESMERALDA BLOGGS   <u>Plaintiff</u>

                              and

                        GORGEOSO JUMPERS PLC   <u>Defendant</u>

<u>PARTICULARS OF CLAIM</u>

1. The Defendants are mail order suppliers of goods and trade from End of
    of the World Lane, Townsley.

2. On 29 February 19__ the Defendants published in the <u>Daily Doings</u> newspaper
    an advertisement in which they offered for sale checked jumpers at a
    price of £15, inclusive of postage and packing.

3. On 1 March 19__ and in response to this advertisement the Plaintiff
    sent a cheque for £15 to the Defendants and enclosed with it a letter
    ordering a checked jumper as described and illustrated in the advertise-
    ment.

4. On 26 March 19__ the Plaintiff received in the post a striped cardigan
    which had been sent by the Defendants.

5. On 1 April 19__ the Plaintiff posted the striped cardigan back to the
    Defendants and enclosed with it a letter requesting a refund and the
    cost of the postage. The Plaintiff has not received any payment from
    the Defendants.

The Plaintiff claims:

1. The sum of £15.

2. £1 which is the cost of the postage to return the striped cardigan to the
    Defendants.

3. Costs.

Signed ....

Dated ....

IN THE WAVESBANDVILE COUNTY COURT   Case No........

BETWEEN

HELEN HIGHWATER   <u>Plaintiff</u>

and

GERALD CONNER (Trading as CONNER RADIO REPAIRS)   <u>Defendant</u>

<u>PARTICULARS OF CLAIM</u>

1. The Defendant is a repairer of electrical equipment and carries on
    business at Waveband Road, Wavesbandville.

2. On 1 March 19__ the Plaintiff took a Sontachi radio to the Defendant's
    shop and left the radio there to be repaired.

3. On 25 March 19__ the Plaintiff collected the radio from the Defendant's
    shop and was assured by him that it had been repaired. The Plaintiff gave
    the Defendant a cheque for £20 in payment.

4. The Plaintiff discovered later, on 25 March 19__ that the repairs to
    the radio had not been done properly or at all as the radio still was
    not working.

5. The Plaintiff returned to the Defendant's shop on 25 March 19__ and
    asked the Defendant to effect the repairs. This he refused to do.
    The Plaintiff wrote to the Defendant on 1 April 19__ requesting return of
    the £20. The Defendant has not returned the £20.

The Plaintiff claims:

1. £20.

2. Interest under Section 69 of the County Courts Act 1984 at the rate of
    15 per cent per annum from 15 March 19__ to [date of issue of summons]
    and thereafter interest at the same rate up to the date of judgement.

3. Costs.

Signed ....

Dated ....

the court within 14 days of getting the court documents through the post.

If the trader doesn't bother to respond then once the 14 days are up you are entitled to 'judgement'.* The court will let you know when the trader should have received the documents so you will know when their time is up. To get the judgement you must produce your plaint note and fill out another form. The court then notifies the trader that judgement has been entered against them. Hopefully they will then send the money but if they don't see below, p. 212,) as to what to do next.

If they do return the form and make it obvious that they are going to defend, then the court will usually fix a date for both you and the trader to attend there for a 'pre-trial review'. If the court does not do so contact them and ask them why not. If in any doubt as to whether the date set is a pre-trial review or the actual hearing ring up and enquire. A pre-trial review is not the actual hearing but an appointment to sort out preliminary matters. You must go to this unless you have agreed all that has to be agreed with the other side in writing and have agreed that neither of you will go. You must also write to the court to that effect. If you do not turn up, the court may well strike your claim out and although you might be able to persuade them later to put it back again, don't rely on it. At the pre-trial review a number of matters will be sorted out and it will take place in a private room before a court official called the registrar.

If the opposition do not turn up, ask that you be given judgement. Also ask for judgement if the opposition have filed a defence which is completely fatuous. The registrar may well put pressure on them to settle up if it is obvious that you are in the right. If they persist and say that they do have a real defence, demand that they give proper details of it. You in turn may be asked to give more details of your allegations.

You and the opposition can also be asked to show each other what documents you have in your possession which are relevant to the case and not privileged from disclosure. An example of privileged documents are letters between you and your solicitor. (Ask the registrar for guidance if in doubt.) This process is called 'discovery'. In the fictional case against Gorgeoso Jumpers, the documents the consumer would disclose would be the advertise-

---

* If you have requested any sort of redress other than just money, e.g. return of goods, you will have to wait until the pre-trial review.

ment, the cheque if the consumer has got it back, the certificate of posting the cardigan back if the consumer has one, and correspondence detween the consumer and the firm.

If expert witnesses are going to be involved or if a plan of the area or photographs are to be used then it will save expense if the experts' report or the plan or photograph can be accepted as accurate by both sides. That way you avoid the expense of producing two sets of photographs, etc. and also the unnecessary and expensive attendance of witnesses at the hearing can be prevented. The pre-trial review is the place to sort this out and also to eliminate other areas of non-conflict.

Lastly it must be established what sort of hearing there is to be and when. If the claim is for less than £500 the hearing will be an arbitration (except in unusual and difficult circumstances) but if the claim is for more than that you and the opposition may agree to ask for arbitration anyway. If there is to be an arbitration then it must be decided who is to arbitrate as both sides must be in agreement on this issue. The registrar will be prepared to arbitrate free of charge, but if you want someone else to do it you will probably have to pay a large fee. Also, if both sides agree the arbitration could be on documents only, as with a trading association arbitration.

If you know the case will get as far as an actual hearing then before or after the pre-trial review you should start preparing as follows:

- If you've not done so already, write out your own statement of what happened. You will not be allowed to read this out at the hearing but you are permitted to read it to refresh your memory before the case.
- Get your witnesses of 'fact' to do the same. A witness of fact would, for example, be someone who witnessed your conversations with the trader if this is relevant. If someone witnessed what Mr Conner said to Ms Highwater or what Mr Nixon of Wheeler Auto Dealers said to Mr Driver before he bought the car their evidence could be crucial. Make sure the witnesses know that they must attend the hearing; providing a written statement will not be allowed. To encourage them, point out that you can ask that the opposition pay their expenses if you win.
- Do you want or can you get an 'expert' witness? If so, what will be the cost of getting this person involved? You can ask

him/her to prepare a written report to start with, and tell you how much this will cost. Then you can see at the pre-trial review whether the other side will agree the contents so that the expert won't have to attend to give evidence. If the expert does come to the hearing, be prepared for the fact that even if you win the expert might want to charge you more than the court will allow. In the case of Mr Driver's claim against Wheeler Auto Dealers getting an expert mechanic to report on the sorry state of the car could be crucial. Ms Highwater might consider whether there are any radio experts around who could examine the radio and say what has caused its failure to work. However, as her claim is so small this may not be very cost-effective.

The hearing

This will take place either in a public court before a judge or, in the case of arbitration, in private before an arbitrator. If the case is held in court then all the strict legal rules about procedure and admissibility of evidence will apply. The rules are complicated, so take advice first.

An arbitration is much more informal. Everyone sits round a table in an ordinary room and the arbitrator won't wear robes as judges do. The arbitrator will decide how to conduct the hearing and they have a very wide discretion in this respect. When you are asked for your side of the story, keep to the point. If the opposition cross-questions you, stick to your guns. When the other side gives their version then ask to cross-question them. Challenge everything they have said with which you do not agree and ask questions which might discredit their evidence or elicit any points favourable to you.

Example Dialogue.
Mr Wally Driver 'It's right, isn't it, that before I bought the car you told me that it was in excellent condition, had been fully serviced and had no faults?'
Mr Nixon 'Did I really say that?'
Mr Driver 'Yes, you did.'
Mr Nixon 'Well, well, well.'
The Registrar 'Did you make those remarks or not?'
Mr Nixon 'Can't say, can't say. Not after all this time.'
Mr Driver 'Are those the sort of remarks you habitually make to people who might be interested in buying a car from you?'

Mr Nixon (in exasperated tones) 'I am a salesman, you know.'
Mr Driver 'So you could have said something like that?'
Mr Nixon 'Well, I could have said anything.'
Registrar 'I see.'

Mr Nixon's credibility with the registrar might not be too good by this time!

The registrar will be a trained lawyer and should therefore know all about the relevant legislation and case law. However, if you feel up to it, it will do no harm to demonstrate that you too know something on the subject.

The decision will usually be announced on the spot. If you win, ask for costs (see p. 203). If you have lost then you may be asked for costs but you can ask for time to pay.

If the case has been heard by arbitration then you cannot appeal the decision unless the arbitrator has done something really outrageous. If the case has been heard in court then in theory your rights to challenge the decision by going to a higher court are more extensive, but in either situation do not try to take the matter further without advice.

Getting the money

If you won the case or got judgement because the other side didn't bother to defend, then you should get your money without any further ado. But what if you don't? Unlike the criminal court which automatically chases up defaulters and forces them to pay, the County Court will do nothing until you approach them and then they will not take any further action without getting another fee from you.

There are a number of ways of enforcing the judgement and there isn't space here to go into them in detail. However, here are some tips:

You can get the court bailiffs to go round to the traders' premises with the object of seizing their goods, selling them and using the proceeds to pay their fees (which aren't cheap) and your judgement. Frequently the appearance of the bailiff will settle the matter and it is amazing how often traders will delay payment until this point. To get the bailiff on to them you must produce your plaint note to the court, fill out a form and pay another fee. At the moment the fees are 15p per £1 claimed, with a minimum charge of £5 and a maximum of £30. The trader will have to pay this back to you on top of what they already owe.

If this method does not work or if you do not choose to adopt it, you can get the offender brought to court for an 'oral examination'. The object of this is to find out more about the trader's financial situation so you can decide what to do next. They will be told to bring all their trading books, etc. and if they do not turn up they will be given one more chance to come, and could then, if they do not appear, be sent to prison. To get an appointment you must produce your plaint note, fill in a form and pay a fee. Once again the defendant will owe you this on top of everything else. At the examination it is important to obtain details of all bank and building society accounts because you can take money in there by means of a 'garnishee'. It is also important to get details of any salary because you can get an 'attachment of earnings' order in respect of this. You can also get a 'charging order' in respect of any property they own. (If you have the relevant information you can go ahead with these options without an oral examination.)

15.

The consumer on the defensive

So far, we have concentrated on situations where the consumer has taken the offensive. However, there could be occasions where consumers might instead have to defend themselves in an action brought against them by a trader. This could arise where, for a variety of reasons, a consumer has failed to pay a trader's bill. The failure to pay might be accidental or done deliberately in protest at shoddy goods or services, or it might be because the consumer simply cannot afford to pay up.

In this chapter we give some guidance as to what to do in such situations. Sometimes a consumer might come up against the police, if the trader suspected some sort of deliberate dishonesty was involved. But in most situations any action taken against a non-paying consumer would be taken through the civil courts.

When the police are called

On p. 189 we have warned of some tactics consumers might try which might lead to the police being called. But there are situations where a consumer may not be looking for trouble but encounters it anyway. It is all too easy to walk absent-mindedly out of a shop forgetting to pay for something or to order a big meal in a restaurant only to discover when all has been consumed that you have no money to pay. Exceeding a credit limit could also lead the police to your door. What is your legal position if you find yourself in any of these embarrassing situations?

Forgetting to pay

Anyone who walks out of a shop without paying for an item is liable to be arrested for theft of the item in question. Section 1 of the Theft Act 1968 states: 'A person is guilty of theft if he dishonestly appropriates property belonging to another with the intention of permanently depriving the other of it.'

If the case goes to court, therefore, the consumer should not be found guilty of theft unless the prosecution can prove beyond all reasonable doubt that the consumer meant to be dishonest and meant to keep the item without paying for it. So, if what occurred resulted from sheer forgetfulness and not from a deliberate desire to take something and not pay, the consumer is not guilty of theft. Some shops are prepared to listen to reasonable explanations but others prosecute absolutely everyone who walks out without paying. We do not have room here to give comprehensive advice about what to do when arrested. However, do note that anything you say to either the store detective or shop workers or police can be written down and later used in evidence against you. If you are charged with theft you can consult a solicitor under the legal aid scheme and you might also be granted legal aid to be represented in court.

Having no money on you

If you go to pay for an item and find you have no money on you then it is usually a simple matter to return the item and then walk out, albeit somewhat embarrassed! But sometimes this is not possible, e.g. if the item has been consumed, or not easy, e.g. if petrol has just been put into your tank.

It is a criminal offence dishonestly to obtain property belonging to another with the intention of permanently depriving that other of it (Section 15, Theft Act 1968), or by any deception, dishonestly to obtain services from another (Section 1, Theft Act 1978). Also:

A person who knowing that payment on the spot for any goods supplied or service done is required or expected from him, dishonestly makes off without having paid as required or expected and with intent to avoid payment of the amount due shall be guilty of an offence. (Section 3, Theft Act 1978)

It follows that to run off is the worst possible thing to do. Keep calm and remember that you are guilty of criminal behaviour only if you intended all along to obtain the goods or service without paying for them. Explain your dilemma to the trader and try to think of some way of getting the money to them. Is there a nearby friend you can phone or a cash till you could use? Or is there anything, such as a watch, you could offer to leave as security. Get a receipt for the item if you do this. If, despite all your efforts, the police are called then note the advice given above.

Credit crime

If your bank gives you a cheque card to use they may later ask for it back if you become overdrawn. You might not take this seriously and continue to use it, or you might not receive the letter. You might also exceed the limit allowed you on a credit card. Normally such events would, at worst, lead to civil proceedings (see later) but people have been prosecuted. The prosecution would have to prove that the excess use of either card was done with a dishonest intention. The law is complex in this area and you should definitely take legal advice as soon as possible if threatened with a prosecution for a credit crime.

Demands for payment

If the dispute is not a matter for the police but the trader wants you to pay up, they will not rush to the civil court straight away (indeed the court would criticize them if they did), so the hostilities will inevitably start with a letter. The trader will either write direct or go to a debt collection agency or solicitor. If the goods have been bought on credit then a default notice must be served before certain types of punitive action can be taken. In any event you will get a warning as to whether trouble is on the way. The worst possible thing you could do in such a situation is to bury your head in the sand in the hope that the bad news will go away. It won't! If you get a nasty letter it is important to sort things out or you might end up owing even more.

If a letter arrives and you know you do owe the money then it is best to pay up straight away if you can. If you provoke the trader into a court case which you cannot defend you will have to pay their court fee and some solicitors' costs on top of the debt itself. If you know you owe the money but haven't got it, then see below.

If you are not sure whether you should pay or not then try and take advice quickly.

If you accept you owe something but not all of it then it is best to pay what you agree you owe and write to explain why you consider you do not owe the rest. Keep what you say short and to the point and remember your letter will be produced in any later court proceedings (unless you head it 'without prejudice'). It is worth paying the proportion because that way you avoid paying court costs in respect of that amount.

If you are sure you do not owe anything, write back to say this and give a short explanation (with the same point in mind as above), making it clear that any court proceedings will be defended. If you are being unjustly hounded it is worth making a complaint (see p. 175).

If you realize you simply cannot afford to pay, you could offer to pay off the debt by instalments. It is possible that the trader will agree to this as going to court will cost money and the court might well let you pay by instalments anyway. The trader may want details of your financial situation so that they can assess whether your offer is a reasonable one. As you would have to give this information to the court if the matter got that far, you may as well tell them. If an instalment agreement is made it is vital that you keep to what you promised or, if your circumstances become even worse, write and explain and ask for more time. If you default on your side of the deal without explanation the trader will decide you are not to be trusted and will probably rush off to court without delay.

If you cannot cope with the repayments on an HP or hire agreement, then you may wish to put an end to it. See below for your rights in this respect.

Being taken to court

If the trader decides to take you to court then the court will post various documents to you. These will consist of a summons, a copy of the trader's 'particulars of claim' and a form of 'admission, defence or counterclaim' which you must complete to say whether you admit the claim or not and whether you wish to claim against the trader for anything (called a counterclaim). You have *14 days* in which to fill out this form and send it back to the court, otherwise the trader can get immediate judgement against you.

Defending the claim

There is no point in defending if you do not have a defence. This will only add to the costs you will end up paying. If you are not sure what to do then take advice. If you do decide to defend, then you will see a section of the form the court has sent you headed 'Defence' with two questions:

'Do you dispute the plaintiff's claim or any part of it? YES/NO'
'If so how much do you dispute and what are your reasons?'

When answering the second question keep what you say brief and to the point but make sure you do specify why you are defending. If you do not do so or if you say something that does not amount to any defence in law then the trader can ask the court for judgement on the basis that you have no genuine answer to their claim.

■ (There is a claim against a consumer for goods delivered and not paid for.)
1. I dispute the whole of the Plaintiffs' claim.
2. On 1 April I wrote to the Plaintiffs and asked them to send me a checked jumper but I never received any such jumper from them.

Once the consumer's defence is received the next stage will probably be the pre-trial review (see p. 209). Use this opportunity if you wish to demand more details of the allegations against you. If these are utterly fatuous you can ask that the claim be dismissed forthwith. If you are being sued for less than £500 the case will be referred automatically to arbitration. If you are being sued for more then £500 there is a space on the form for you to request arbitration if you wish to do so. See p. 211 for advice about the hearing.

Counterclaiming

If you consider that you have a valid claim against a trader who has taken you to court you can take this opportunity to 'counterclaim' against them. There is a space on the form for you to set out your allegations against the trader and you should fill this out in the same way as if you were the plaintiff and then act as if the counterclaim was your particulars of claim (see p. 205).

Admission

If you accept that you owe some or all of the money the trader is claiming from you, then you must admit this on the relevant part of the form. There is a place for you to ask the court to permit you to pay off the debt by instalments and later you will be asked what amount of instalments you are offering. If you want to do this you must fill out a section revealing how much money you have. A copy of what you have put on the form will be sent to the trader by the court and they will be asked if your offer is acceptable. If it isn't, there will have to be a hearing to sort this out. If it is, judgement will be entered on that basis and as long as you keep to your side of the bargain that's the last you'll hear of it. Unfortunately, having let things get this far, you will have to pay not only the debt but the trader's court fee for starting the case off and, if they used a solicitor, that person's fees for preparing the documents. The latter cannot be more than a fixed amount, and if the claim is less that £25 no legal fees can be claimed. If the claim is for £25 to £250 then the sum is currently £18 and from £250 to £600 it is £24. If you fail to keep up your payments further action (see later) will probably be taken against you, thus adding further solicitors' and court costs to what you already owe. If you find that you can no longer pay the instalments you offered because your financial situation has worsened, then write to the trader or the court and try to get the instalments reduced. Don't just give up and leave it.

The end of the road

If there is a judgement against you and you do not pay up, the trader can get the bailiff on to you. If by some mishap you never got the court documents you could ask the bailiff for the court number and then rush along there and ask for a chance to defend yourself. If you did know all about it then now is the time to pay up if you can.

The bailiff is allowed to take away all your possessions and sell them to pay the judgement plus the cost of the sale. You are allowed to keep £100 worth (at the moment) of clothes and bedding belonging to you and your family and up to £150 worth (at the moment) of tools of your trade. The bailiff cannot seize goods belonging to anyone else and that includes goods which you are hiring or buying on hire purchase.

There are a number of other things that can be done to you if you do not pay (see p. 212).

Index of statutory instruments

Cases index

Statutes index

Index

RIGHTS AT WORK
JEREMY McMULLEN
Second Edition

Completely revised and greatly expanded, this
well-known, authoritative guide to employment
law explains and shows how to use workers'
rights – it covers everything from unfair
dismissal to secondary action, redundancy to
equal rights. All the major changes introduced
by the last government are here, together with
suggestions about how to fight them.

The book supersedes the author's earlier
Employment Law Under the Tories.

'Easily the most accurate, comprehensive and
best-written explanation of employment law
rights designed for union activists; every shop
steward will want a copy.' *Industrial Relations
Review and Report*

560 pages
0 86104 730 3   £7.95 paperback

THE COHABITATION HANDBOOK

A Woman's Guide to the Law
ANNE BOTTOMLEY, KATHERINE
GIEVE, GAY MOON and ANGELA
WEIR·
Second Edition, revised and updated

This new edition, completely revised and
updated, is a practical guide to the law for
women who are living with someone without
being married. It covers such issues as whose
name to take; whose place the rented or bought
home is; homelessness, domestic violence; the
cost of living together; the problems of bringing
up children; and, in addition, offers some very
useful legal advice and further reading.

'A practical and straightforward guide.'
Tribune

256 pages
0 86104 793 1   £5.50 paperback

USING THE MEDIA
DENIS McSHANE

Highly acclaimed, this handbook shows how to
get your message across in the press and on
radio and TV, and explains how to make a
success of press releases, phone-ins,
interviews, news conferences and much more.
  Using the Media has a comprehensive
directory of daily papers, television and radio
stations, trade union journals and socialist
newspapers in Britain and Ireland.

  'Concentrated, comprehensive.' *Guardian*
  'An excellent handbook.' *New Statesman*
  'An invaluable reference book.' *Tribune*

224 pages
0 86104 089 9   £4.50 paperback

PENSIONS
SUE WARD

Demystifying another highly technical subject,
Sue Ward's readable manual comprehensively
explains all you need to know about pensions:
the different schemes, financial arrangements
and trade union participation, and more.

'Clearly set out, and covers everything of
importance. The job could not have been done
better.' *Labour Research*

272 pages
0 86104 333 2   £4.95 paperback

YOUR JOB IN THE EIGHTIES
A Woman's Guide to New
Technology
URSULA HUWS

A manual for action for women workers faced
with the threat of new technology.

   'Timely and readable book... consciousness-
raising.' *New Socialist*
   'Fresh and fascinating.' *Morning Star*

128 pages. Illustrated
0 86104 365 0   £2.50 paperback

A-Z OF MEETINGS
How they Work and How to Improve them
SUE WARD

Foxed by the rules? Exasperated by points of
order? Then *A-Z of Meetings* is for you. This
book is for everyone who wants to make the
most of running or attending meetings –
whether at a trade union branch, political
group, community campaign or tenants'
association.

A-Z of Meetings covers
- constitutions
- standing orders
- alternative rules
- running a meeting
- alternative approaches
- being a conference delegate
- running a conference
- the language and etiquette of meetings

Sue Ward's previous books include
Organising Things and *Pensions*, both
published by Pluto Press.

224 pages
0 86104 780 X £3.95 paperback

ORGANISING THINGS
A Guide to Successful Political Action
SUE WARD

Organising Things is the first comprehensive guide to practical political action. Packed with information and handy checklists, this book takes the tears out of organizing public meetings – how to chair them, how to steward them; marches and demonstrations – how to plan them, how to deal with the police; lobbies – how to arrange mass events; petitions – how to get people to sign; conferences – what to provide and where to book; festivals, fetes and bazaars – how to finance them and what to lay on.

The book shows how to get funds, publicity, help and information. Sue Ward explains how to design and distribute leaflets and posters, and develop your own ideas for publicity. This book tells you all you need to know about the law, and how to cope with disasters.

'... useful, practical handbook, carefully arranged' *Community Work*
'It deserves to be on the shelf of every activist.' *Peace News*

272 pages
0 86104 799 0   £4.95 paperback

INDUSTRIAL TRIBUNALS
How to Take a Case, How to Win it
JOHN McILROY

Knowing how to prepare and present a good case for an industrial tribunal can make the difference between success and failure or the amount paid in compensation. *Industrial Tribunals* is the most detailed step-by-step guide available to making claims against employers for dismissal, redundancy and discrimination.

272 pages
0 86104 368 5   £5.95 paperback

WOMEN AND HARASSMENT AT WORK
NATHALIE HADJIFOTIOU

This is the first detailed guide to tackling sexual harassment at work. It is packed full of practical advice, ideas and examples for campaigning and negotiating in both union and non-union workplaces. It explains where to get help and how to use the law.

208 pages
0 86104 729 X   £3.95 paperback

Pluto books are available through your local bookshop. In case of difficulty contact Pluto to find out local stockists or to obtain catalogues/leaflets (telephone 01-482 1973).
    If all else fails write to:

Pluto Press Limited
Freepost (no stamp required)
105A Torriano Avenue
London NW5 1YP